The Accent Diet

A Daily Program for Improving Your
American English Pronunciation

Blythe J. Musteric, MA TESOL
Marc J. Musteric, MA East Asian Languages

Ovient, Inc.
Sunnyvale, CA

The Accent Diet

A Daily Program for Improving Your American English Pronunciation

Blythe J. Musteric & Marc J. Musteric

Ovient, Inc., 440 N. Wolfe Rd., Sunnyvale, CA 94085

Visit our website at www.ovient.com.

Library of Congress Control Number: 2013908804

ISBN-13: 978-0-9894305-0-0

Printed in the United States of America

Book Design by Stuart L. Silberman
Cover Design by Stuart L. Silberman
Editing by Amy L. Lehman and Rachel Klein

First Edition: August 2013

10 9 8 7 6 5 4 3 2 1

Contents

Who Should Use This Book?

This book was created for intermediate and advanced speakers of English who feel that their accents create a barrier to communication with their coworkers or customers. If you are often asked to repeat yourself when speaking, you need this book. If you speak English with the same patterns and sounds that you use in your first language, you need this book.

The reason your coworkers, friends, or customers have difficulty understanding your English is because you are probably not speaking in the patterns that native English speakers use. In order to change your speech patterns, you will need to change how you speak. This book will help you learn how to change these patterns.

Why Is This Program Called the Accent "Diet"?

We use the word "diet" because improving your accent is very similar to the process you use to lose weight. If you want to lose weight, you must eat well and exercise every day. If you want to change your pronunciation or learn an American accent, you must study and practice every day. Just as a person needs to learn healthy eating habits and follow them consistently in order to lose weight, you need to learn clear speaking habits and continue to practice these habits over a long period of time to change your pronunciation.

How Is This Program Different from Other Accent or Pronunciation Programs?

Many accent books on the market today teach you important pronunciation rules, but rules are not enough. You need to learn how to create new habits. This book teaches you how to change your behavior. You can buy a cookbook and read about healthy recipes, but this will not help you improve your eating habits unless you actually prepare healthy food in your kitchen. This book will not only give you the rules you need, but it will also guide you through daily practice activities so that you create new habits. In addition, you can listen to audio for all practice pages at www.myovient.com.

This book is also different in another key way. Instead of giving you many rules to remember, this book will focus on just three Accent Diet™ basics. Because the rules are simple, you are more likely to remember them.

Do I Need to Study Every Day?

Yes. The key to changing your accent or pronunciation is changing your speaking habits, and the only way to change your speaking habits is to practice every day. If you want to improve, you will need to add Accent Diet™ study time to your schedule every day. If you are like most professionals, you are very busy and do not have a lot of extra time. However, if you want to improve your pronunciation, you need to approach this program as if you were preparing for the New York City Marathon or a performance at Carnegie Hall. You need to practice every day, and you need to practice whenever you speak English. To use the diet analogy again, you need to change your behavior not just for now, but for the rest of your life.

How Do I Use the Recordings?

Every practice page has corresponding audio files that you can use to practice. Go to www.myovient.com and type the audio code into the search box. Here are some ways to use the audio:

1) Listen to the audio and repeat what you hear while looking at the textbook.
2) Pronounce the words at the same time as the speaker while looking at the textbook.
3) Listen to the audio and repeat what you hear without looking at the textbook.
4) Pronounce the words at the same time as the speaker without looking at the textbook.

A Note to Teachers and Language Coaches:

We created this textbook because many of the pronunciation books on the market today focus primarily on discrete sounds and small changes that do little to change the speech patterns of non-native speakers. Many of the textbooks teach rules to memorize and fail to focus on the "feeling" of English, which we have found to be a better way to change behavior. The learners who have used our method have seen positive results in their intelligibility both in the workplace and in their social lives.

If you are familiar with the standard principles of teaching pronunciation, you will find it easy to teach from this book. We recommend that you avoid focusing on discrete sounds (e.g. /l/ and /r/) until Lesson 9. We strongly believe that clear speech can be achieved quickly if learners focus on the first three lessons of this book before practicing discrete sounds. (Some learners will insist that you help them with discrete sounds from the beginning of the course because this is what "pronunciation improvement" means to them. If you feel that this will help motivate the learner to stay interested in the class, then instruct them as needed.)

When planning your classes, focus on completing one book lesson per week. This will give the learners time to complete one practice page on their own per day. (Of course, this will depend on how many hours you have for the entire course. We have had success using this book in courses with 24 contact hours.) Begin the lesson by teaching the key concept. Next, choose a few exercises from the lesson and practice as a class. Finally, give learners an opportunity to speak freely through role plays, debates, speeches, etc. while focusing on the objective of that chapter. Give feedback as necessary, but do not stop to correct problems beyond the chapter you are working on. You should assign the practice pages as outside work.

We recommend using a voice recorder to record and play back samples of the learners' speech. Recordings serve two functions: 1) learners are more likely to change if they can hear their mistakes, and 2) you can use the recordings to benchmark the learners' successes.

The Appendix is filled with additional pages that can be used as needed, depending on the learners. You might want to go through these pages at the beginning of the course and refer to them as you move through the book. We recommend using the "Warm Ups" at the beginning of every class session.

LESSON PAGES

Below is an illustration of the first page of Lesson 1. The descriptions in the boxes explain what you will find on each LESSON PAGE and how to interact with each lesson.

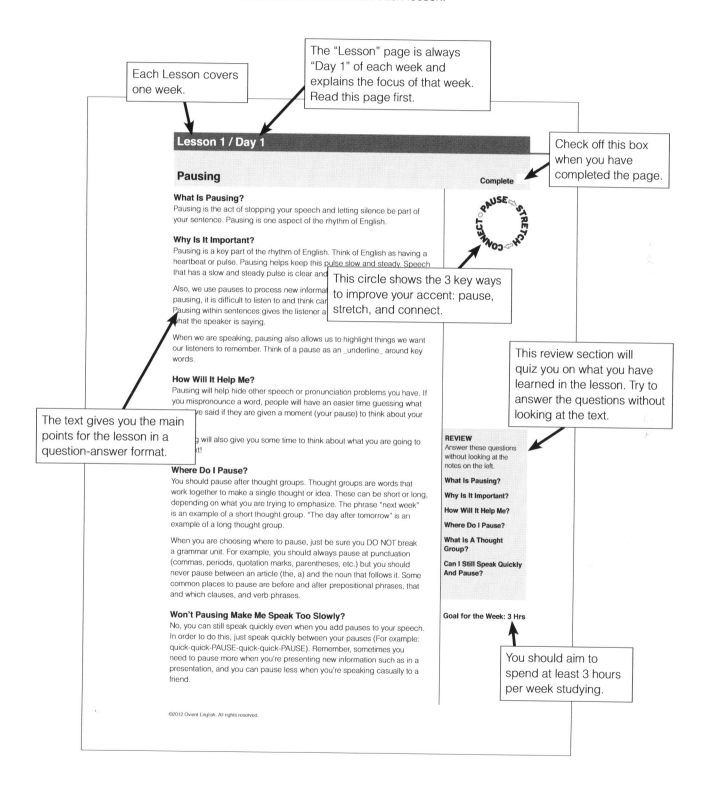

Each Lesson covers one week.

The "Lesson" page is always "Day 1" of each week and explains the focus of that week. Read this page first.

Check off this box when you have completed the page.

Lesson 1 / Day 1

Pausing

Complete

What Is Pausing?
Pausing is the act of stopping your speech and letting silence be part of your sentence. Pausing is one aspect of the rhythm of English.

Why Is It Important?
Pausing is a key part of the rhythm of English. Think of English as having a heartbeat or pulse. Pausing helps keep this pulse slow and steady. Speech that has a slow and steady pulse is clear and

Also, we use pauses to process new informa... pausing, it is difficult to listen to and think car... Pausing within sentences gives the listener a... what the speaker is saying.

When we are speaking, pausing also allows us to highlight things we want our listeners to remember. Think of a pause as an _underline_ around key words.

How Will It Help Me?
Pausing will help hide other speech or pronunciation problems you have. If you mispronounce a word, people will have an easier time guessing what ...ve said if they are given a moment (your pause) to think about your

...g will also give you some time to think about what you are going to ...kt!

This circle shows the 3 key ways to improve your accent: pause, stretch, and connect.

The text gives you the main points for the lesson in a question-answer format.

Where Do I Pause?
You should pause after thought groups. Thought groups are words that work together to make a single thought or idea. These can be short or long, depending on what you are trying to emphasize. The phrase "next week" is an example of a short thought group. "The day after tomorrow" is an example of a long thought group.

When you are choosing where to pause, just be sure you DO NOT break a grammar unit. For example, you should always pause at punctuation (commas, periods, quotation marks, parentheses, etc.) but you should never pause between an article (the, a) and the noun that follows it. Some common places to pause are before and after prepositional phrases, that and which clauses, and verb phrases.

Won't Pausing Make Me Speak Too Slowly?
No, you can still speak quickly even when you add pauses to your speech. In order to do this, just speak quickly between your pauses (For example: quick-quick-PAUSE-quick-quick-PAUSE). Remember, sometimes you need to pause more when you're presenting new information such as in a presentation, and you can pause less when you're speaking casually to a friend.

This review section will quiz you on what you have learned in the lesson. Try to answer the questions without looking at the text.

REVIEW
Answer these questions without looking at the notes on the left.

What Is Pausing?

Why Is It Important?

How Will It Help Me?

Where Do I Pause?

What Is A Thought Group?

Can I Still Speak Quickly And Pause?

Goal for the Week: 3 Hrs

You should aim to spend at least 3 hours per week studying.

How to Use This Book

PRACTICE PAGES

Below is an illustration of the first practice page of Lesson 1. The descriptions in the boxes explain what you will find on each practice page and how you should interact with it.

There are 7 "Practice" days each week. On the first day of each week, you will read the lesson and complete one practice page.

If you see an "audio" number, type the number in the search box at www.myovient.com to find audio files that match the lesson.

Check off this box when you have completed the page.

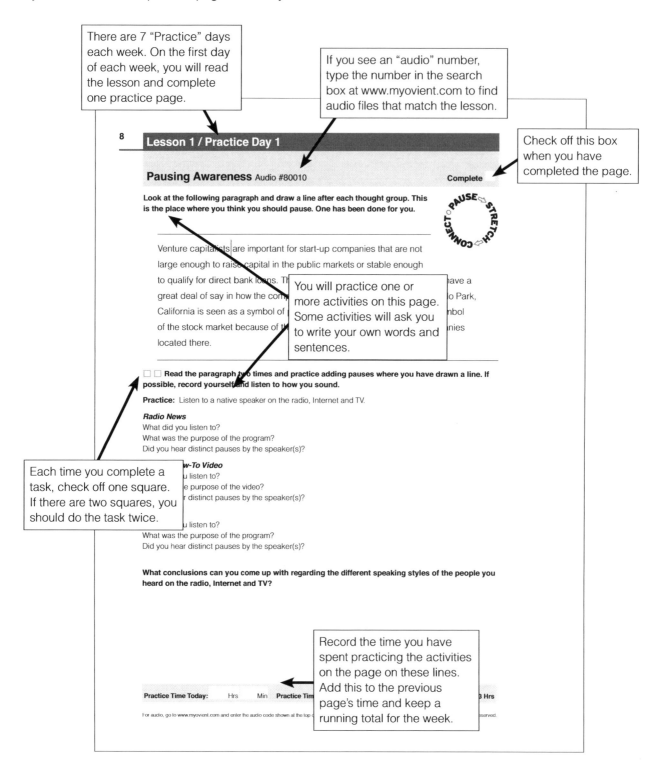

8

Lesson 1 / Practice Day 1

Pausing Awareness Audio #80010   Complete

Look at the following paragraph and draw a line after each thought group. This is the place where you think you should pause. One has been done for you.

Venture capitalists are important for start-up companies that are not large enough to raise capital in the public markets or stable enough to qualify for direct bank loans. Th[...] [...]ave a great deal of say in how the com[...] [...]o Park, California is seen as a symbol of [...] [...]nbol of the stock market because of t[...] [...]nies located there.

You will practice one or more activities on this page. Some activities will ask you to write your own words and sentences.

☐ ☐ Read the paragraph two times and practice adding pauses where you have drawn a line. If possible, record yourself and listen to how you sound.

Practice: Listen to a native speaker on the radio, Internet and TV.

Radio News
What did you listen to?
What was the purpose of the program?
Did you hear distinct pauses by the speaker(s)?

[...]w-To Video
[...]u listen to?
[...]e purpose of the video?
[...]r distinct pauses by the speaker(s)?

[...]u listen to?
What was the purpose of the program?
Did you hear distinct pauses by the speaker(s)?

What conclusions can you come up with regarding the different speaking styles of the people you heard on the radio, Internet and TV?

Each time you complete a task, check off one square. If there are two squares, you should do the task twice.

Record the time you have spent practicing the activities on the page on these lines. Add this to the previous page's time and keep a running total for the week.

Practice Time Today: Hrs   Min   **Practice Tim**[...] [...]3 Hrs

For audio, go to www.myovient.com and enter the audio code shown at the top [...] [...]eserved.

Pre-Assessment

In order to measure your improvement after you have completed the Accent Diet™, you will need to compare a sample of your speech from before and after you complete the program. Read the paragraph below, record your voice, and save your recording.

Read this paragraph in your natural speaking voice. Do not try to make any adjustments to your accent. This recording will serve as the base for measuring your learning. (If you are working with an instructor, be sure to give this recording to him or her before you start your class.)

Do you ever look around you and wonder whether you are dressed appropriately for your job? Do you notice men coming to work without a tie and think they're underdressed? Dress codes in many companies today are relaxed, and in many cases "business-casual" clothing is normal. Khaki pants and shirts without ties are common and acceptable. This is especially true in professions where employees are not in face-to-face contact with customers. Some employees in more relaxed areas of business can even go to work in jeans and t-shirts. Even if their workplace requires more formal clothing, like suits and ties, they might have one day a week when employees can relax and dress down, usually called "casual Friday." The best way to understand how to dress for your workplace is to analyze what your coworkers are wearing. Whatever your company requires, be sure to wear clothing that feels good. That way, even if you don't like the dress code, at least you'll be comfortable!

Before You Start

You need a dictionary to help you improve your pronunciation. (Paper, electronic, or Web-based dictionaries are all okay.) Look for a dictionary with a clear pronunciation guide. Most dictionaries use the International Phonetic Alphabet (IPA), but some use their own unique guide. As you are studying the Accent Diet™, it is important that you use a dictionary to check the pronunciation of words you do not know.

Introduction to Part One

Changing your pronunciation is about changing your behavior. To be successful, you must first master the basic steps in lessons one through three. You must learn to:

PAUSE—STRETCH—CONNECT™

Part One of the Accent Diet™ will help you master these Accent Diet™ Basics. You should be able to master these steps in about three weeks. Once you master the Basics, you should begin to notice a difference in your life. You should notice that your friends and coworkers ask you to repeat yourself less frequently, people are more interested in talking with you, and life in an English speaking country is a bit easier. If you are not noticing these changes, then you need to spend more time practicing.

Part Two of the Accent Diet™ includes Lessons 4 through 11. These are the Accent Diet™ Advanced Topics. Once you have completely mastered the Accent Diet™ Basics, you may want to explore these Advanced Topics. However, you should not focus on the Advanced Topics without first mastering the Basics.

Pausing

Complete ☐

What Is Pausing?

Pausing is the act of stopping your speech and allowing silence to be part of your sentence. Pausing is one aspect of the rhythm of English.

Why Is It Important?

Pausing is a key part of the rhythm of English. Think of English as having a heartbeat or pulse. Pausing helps keep this pulse slow and steady. Speech that has a slow and steady pulse is clear and sounds confident.

Also, we use pauses to process new information. Without pausing, your speech may be difficult to understand. Pausing within sentences gives the listener a chance to think carefully about what the speaker is saying.

Pausing also allows us to highlight things we want our listeners to remember. Think of a pause as an _underline_ around key words.

How Will It Help Me?

Pausing will help hide other speech and pronunciation problems you have. If you mispronounce a word, people will have an easier time guessing what you have said if they are given a moment (your pause) to think about your word.

Pausing will also give you some time to think about what you are going to say next!

Where Do I Pause?

You should pause after thought groups. Thought groups are words that work together to form a single thought or idea. Thought groups can be short or long, depending on what you are trying to emphasize. The phrase "next week" is an example of a short thought group. "The day after tomorrow" is an example of a long thought group.

When you are choosing where to pause, just be sure you DO NOT break a grammar unit. For example, you should always pause at punctuation (commas, periods, quotation marks, parentheses, etc.), but you should never pause between an article (the, a) and the noun that follows it. Some common places to pause are before and after prepositional phrases, before "that" and "which" clauses, and between items in a list.

Will Pausing Make My Speech Too Slow?

No, you can still speak quickly even when you add pauses to your speech. In order to do this, just speak quickly between your pauses (For example: quick-quick-PAUSE-quick-quick-PAUSE). You need to pause more when you are presenting new information and pause less when you are speaking casually to a friend.

REVIEW
Answer these questions without looking at the notes on the left.

What is pausing?

Why is it important?

How will it help me?

Where do I pause?

What is a thought Group?

Can I still speak quickly and pause?

Goal for the Week: 3 Hrs

Pausing Awareness Audio #80010

Look at the following paragraph and draw a line after each thought group. This is the place where you think you should pause. One has been done for you.

Venture capitalists|are important for start-up companies|that are not large enough to raise capital in the public markets|or stable enough to qualify|for direct bank loans. The investors in these companies|usually have a great deal of say|in how the companies will be run. Sand Hill Road|in Menlo Park, California|is seen as a symbol of private capital,|just as Wall Street|is a symbol of the stock market|because of the large number|of venture capital companies located there.

☐ ☐ **Read the paragraph two times and practice adding pauses where you have drawn a line. If possible, record yourself and listen to how you sound.**

Practice: Listen to a native speaker on the radio, Internet and TV.

Radio News
What did you listen to?
What was the purpose of the program?
Did you hear distinct pauses by the speaker(s)?

Internet How-To Video
What did you listen to?
What was the purpose of the video?
Did you hear distinct pauses by the speaker(s)?

TV Show
What did you listen to?
What was the purpose of the program?
Did you hear distinct pauses by the speaker(s)?

What conclusions can you make regarding the different speaking styles of the people you heard on the radio, Internet and TV?

Practice Time Today:	Hrs	Min	Practice Time this Week:	Hrs	Min	Goal for the Week: 3 Hrs

Pausing Practice Audio #80020

Complete ☐

Practice reading these numbers and sentences. Pause at the end of each line break. Read each one five times.

PAUSE ⇨ STRETCH ⇩ CONNECT ○

☐ ☐ ☐ ☐ ☐
3 + (3 x 2) = 9
three plus
three times two
equals nine

☐ ☐ ☐ ☐ ☐
(3 + 3) x 2 = 12
three plus three
times two
equals twelve

☐ ☐ ☐ ☐ ☐
(10 − 3) x 7 = 49
ten minus three
times seven
equals forty nine

☐ ☐ ☐ ☐ ☐
10 − (3 x 7) = -11
ten minus
three times seven
equals negative eleven

These examples show you that sometimes pauses can change the meaning of a sentence or phrase.

☐ ☐ ☐ ☐ ☐
555-524-1649
five five five
five two four
one six four nine

☐ ☐ ☐ ☐ ☐
5555-241-649
five five five five
two four one
six four nine

☐ ☐ ☐ ☐ ☐
"Tom," said Cathy, "is mean."
Tom
said Cathy
is mean. (Cathy thinks Tom is mean.)

☐ ☐ ☐ ☐ ☐
Tom said Cathy is mean.
Tom said
Cathy is mean. (Tom thinks Cathy is mean.)

☐ ☐ ☐ ☐ ☐
I would like to buy a car, phone, and house.
I would like to buy
a car
phone
and house.

☐ ☐ ☐ ☐ ☐
I would like to buy a car phone and house.
I would like to buy
a car phone
and house.

☐ ☐ ☐ ☐ ☐
Do you want a soup or salad?
Do you want
a soup
or salad?

☐ ☐ ☐ ☐ ☐
Do you want a super salad?
Do you want
a super salad?

Practice Time Today:	Hrs	Min	**Practice Time this Week:**	Hrs	Min	**Goal for the Week: 3 Hrs**

For audio, go to www.myovient.com and enter the audio code shown at the top of this page.

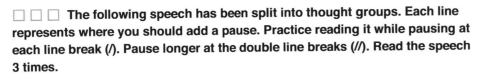

Lesson 1 / Practice Day 3

Pausing Practice Audio #80030

Complete ☐

☐ ☐ ☐ **The following speech has been split into thought groups. Each line represents where you should add a pause. Practice reading it while pausing at each line break (/). Pause longer at the double line breaks (//). Read the speech 3 times.**

What is your future?/
Will you spend your life/
working for someone else?/
Or,//

are you brave enough/
to start your own business?//

Starting your own business/
requires courage,/
perseverance,/
and optimism.//

Do you have/
what it takes?//

First,/
you need courage./
Without courage,/
you will fail.//

Forget what your friends are doing/
in their high-paid jobs/
Forget that your parents told you/
to find a stable job./
To start your own business,/
you must be strong,/
you must be fearless,/
and you must be brave.//

You need courage.//

Second,/
you must have perseverance.//
When you start your business,/
you will have problems./
You will face challenges./
You will want to quit./
Don't!//

To be successful,/
you must persevere.//

Finally,/
you must be optimistic.//

Don't think about failure./
Instead,/
focus on success.//

When you make mistakes,/
learn from them./
When something you try doesn't work,/
think about how you can fix it,/
then move on.//

Optimists find opportunities.//

So,/
do you have it?//

Are you courageous?//

Will you persevere?//

Can you remain optimistic/
in the face of adversity?//

Shhhh,/
don't answer.//

Instead,/
go start your business!///

Practice Time Today:	Hrs	Min	Practice Time this Week:	Hrs	Min	Goal for the Week: 3 Hrs

Pausing Practice Audio #80040

Complete ☐

Write a self-introduction. Include your name, job title, the languages you speak, where you grew up, and your interests. Write it out so that each thought group is on a separate line as shown below.

Example:

My name is/
Maggie/
Lim. /
I am a software engineer/
at a company in Sunnyvale./

I speak Chinese,/
Japanese,/
and English./
I grew up/
in Singapore/
and now live/
in the United States./

When you introduce yourself, you should add frequent pauses to your speech because most of your information will be new to the listener.

Write your self-introduction here:

_____

_____

_____

_____

_____

_____

_____

_____

_____

Practice Time Today:	Hrs	Min	**Practice Time this Week:**	Hrs	Min	**Goal for the Week: 3 Hrs**

Pausing Practice Audio #80050   **Complete** ☐

Read these sentences five times each. Pause at the end of each line break.

☐ ☐ ☐ ☐ ☐
The Tech Museum/
in San Jose/
offers visitors/
a chance to see/
how technology works./

☐ ☐ ☐ ☐ ☐
On April 30,/
1993,/
CERN announced/
that the World Wide Web/
would be free to anyone./

☐ ☐ ☐ ☐ ☐
Even today,/
there are fewer women/
who work in software engineering/
than in other professions./

☐ ☐ ☐ ☐ ☐
It is a well-known fact/
that social interaction/
is important/
for our health./

☐ ☐ ☐ ☐ ☐
The meetings we had/
over the course of 2 years/
were very useful/
for the development/
of our product./

☐ ☐ ☐ ☐ ☐
The largest concentration/
of wind turbines/
in the world/
is near Highway 580./

☐ ☐ ☐ ☐ ☐
Moore's Law says/
that the number of transistors/
that can be placed/
on an integrated circuit/
doubles every two years./

☐ ☐ ☐ ☐ ☐
Highway billboards/
are a great way for hotels/
to get last-minute customers./

☐ ☐ ☐ ☐ ☐
Cloud computing systems/
allow you to access your files/
from anywhere./

Write your own sentences using this pattern and practice them five times each.

☐ ☐ ☐ ☐ ☐   ☐ ☐ ☐ ☐ ☐

_____   _____

_____   _____

_____   _____

_____   _____

☐ **Extra Practice:** Listen to a speaker on TV or Online. Write down one sentence and mark the pauses that you hear.

Sentence: _____

Who did you listen to? _____

Practice Time Today:	Hrs	Min	Practice Time this Week:	Hrs	Min	Goal for the Week: 3 Hrs

Pausing Practice Audio #80060

Complete ☐

These sentences can be read with pauses at different places. (The pauses highlight the key message.) Pause at each slash mark. Read each sentence two times.

☐ ☐ You can join us / on Friday / if you want.
☐ ☐ You can join us on Friday / if you want.

☐ ☐ If you don't back up your computer, / you may find yourself / in a terrible situation.
☐ ☐ If you don't back up your computer, / you may find yourself in a terrible situation.

☐ ☐ They said the meeting / is rescheduled / for Monday.
☐ ☐ They said the meeting / is rescheduled for Monday.
☐ ☐ They said the meeting is rescheduled / for Monday.

☐ ☐ Francis thought / her invention / would change the world.
☐ ☐ Francis thought / her invention would change the world.
☐ ☐ Francis thought her invention / would change the world.

☐ ☐ The warning signal / is a blinking light / on the dashboard.
☐ ☐ The warning signal / is a blinking light on the dashboard.
☐ ☐ The warning signal is a blinking light / on the dashboard.

Write a sentence at each number. Copy each sentence three times and add different pauses to each sentence. Read each sentence two times.

1. _____
   a) ☐ ☐ _____
   b) ☐ ☐ _____
   c) ☐ ☐ _____

2. _____
   a) ☐ ☐ _____
   b) ☐ ☐ _____
   c) ☐ ☐ _____

3. _____
   a) ☐ ☐ _____
   b) ☐ ☐ _____
   c) ☐ ☐ _____

| Practice Time Today: | Hrs | Min | Practice Time this Week: | Hrs | Min | Goal for the Week: 3 Hrs |

For audio, go to www.myovient.com and enter the audio code shown at the top of this page.

Pausing Practice Audio #80070

☐ ☐ ☐ **Read this paragraph three times. Pause quickly at single slash marks and pause longer at double slash marks.**

Silicon Valley / is in the southern part / of the San Francisco Bay Area / in Northern California. // The term originally referred / to the region's large number / of silicon chip innovators / and manufacturers // but eventually came to refer / to all the high-tech businesses / in the area. // Despite the development / of other high-tech economic centers / throughout the United States, // Silicon Valley continues to be / the leading high-tech center / because of its large number of engineers / and venture capitalists. //

☐ ☐ ☐ **Write a paragraph about your hometown or the town you live in now. Add single and double slash marks to represent pauses. Read the paragraph three times.**

_____

_____

_____

_____

_____

_____

_____

_____

☐ **Speaking Practice:** Tell someone about your hometown (or look in the mirror and tell yourself). Add pauses while you speak.

Reminder: Add an alarm on your daily calendar to remind yourself to pause. Set it to go off once or twice an hour. Every time you hear the beep, remind yourself to pause when you speak.

Practice Time Today:	Hrs	Min	Practice Time this Week:	Hrs	Min	Goal for the Week: 3 Hrs

Stretching

Complete ☐

What Is Stretching?
Stretching is the act of lengthening the sound of word endings. Stretching is one aspect of the rhythm of English.

Why Is It Important?
Stretching is important because it enables your listener to understand your words clearly. Word endings are very important in English, and if you do not spend enough time on the endings of your words, your listeners will have trouble understanding you.

Where Do I Stretch?
You should stretch the final vowel sound of the last word in each thought group. (See Lesson 1 for information about thought groups.) For example, you should stretch the "a" sound in *back* (baaaack) and the "er" sound in *trainer* (traineeeer).

How Do I Stretch Words That End in a Silent E?
When a word ends in a "vowel + consonant + e," the "e" is silent. You should stretch the vowel before the consonant. For example, stretch the "a" in the word face (faaaace).

Will My Speech Sound Strange If I Stretch the Sounds?
No, it will not sound strange to native speakers. (However, *you* might think you sound strange because you are not used to it.) If you pay close attention to native speakers' words, you will notice that they stretch words very often.

What Is the Difference Between Stress and Stretching?
When you stress a word, you make it longer, louder, and higher pitched. When you stretch a word, you just hold it longer. For example, in the word *finally*, you should stress the first part of the word: FINally. Stretching, on the other hand, only applies to the final vowel sound of the last word in a thought group. When the word finally is the last word in a thought group, you "stress" the "i" and "stretch" the "y": FINally—. (Stress is covered in more detail in Lessons 4 and 6.)

How Long Should I Stretch the Sounds?
As you practice pronouncing your word endings in this chapter, you need to stretch the words longer than what is natural or normal for native speakers. It is okay to exaggerate! Doing this will help you change your habits. Once you begin to stretch your words without thinking about it, you can shorten the words a little bit. (Remember, if it does not feel strange at the beginning, you are probably not stretching enough!)

As you change your speech and try things like stretching, your speech will feel strange. If it feels strange, you are doing it correctly!

REVIEW
Answer these questions without looking at the notes on the left.

What is stretching?

Why is it important?

Where do I stretch?

How do I stretch words that end in a silent "e"?

Will my speech sound strange if I stretch the sounds?

What is the difference between stress and stretching?

How long should I stretch the sounds?

Goal for the Week: 3 Hrs

Stretching Practice Audio #80080

Complete ☐

Read each phrase three times. Stretch the final vowel sound at the end of each phrase.

☐ ☐ ☐ in the next da—y
☐ ☐ ☐ will launch in a wee—k
☐ ☐ ☐ what vendors can do for you—
☐ ☐ ☐ it's oka—y
☐ ☐ ☐ give it to the tea—m
☐ ☐ ☐ they've taken contro—l
☐ ☐ ☐ what they talk abou—t
☐ ☐ ☐ in the da—rk
☐ ☐ ☐ still haven't fou—nd

☐ ☐ ☐ get ready to se—ll
☐ ☐ ☐ president of the fi—rm
☐ ☐ ☐ the cost of energy—
☐ ☐ ☐ give it to me—
☐ ☐ ☐ register today—
☐ ☐ ☐ a number of topi—cs
☐ ☐ ☐ need to leverage the we—b
☐ ☐ ☐ get what you wa—nt
☐ ☐ ☐ solutions are neede—d

When a word ends in a "vowel + consonant + e," stretch the vowel before the consonant. The final "e" is silent.

☐ ☐ ☐ have to gi—ve
☐ ☐ ☐ to be do—ne

☐ ☐ ☐ software as a servi—ce
☐ ☐ ☐ give us a quo—te

Think of phrases that you often use in your own speech. Write them here. Practice stretching the final vowel sounds.

☐ ☐ ☐ _____
☐ ☐ ☐ _____
☐ ☐ ☐ _____
☐ ☐ ☐ _____

Practice Time Today: Hrs Min **Practice Time this Week:** Hrs Min **Goal for the Week: 3 Hrs**

Connecting and Stretching Audio #80090

Complete ☐

☐ ☐ ☐ **Read this paragraph aloud. The slashes (/) represent where you should pause, and the dashes (—) represent where you should stretch. Remember to exaggerate your stretching. Read this paragraph three times.**

Silicon Valley— / is in the southern pa—rt / of the San Francisco

Bay Area— / in Northern California— /. The term originally refe—rred / to the

region's large numbe—r / of silicon chip innovato—rs / and manufacture—rs / but

eventually came to refe—r / to all the high-tech businesse—s / in the area— /.

Despite the developme—nt / of other high-tech economic cente—rs / throughout

the United Sta—tes /, Silicon Valley— / continues to be— / the leading high-

tech cente—r / because of its large numbe—r / of enginee—rs / and venture

capitali—sts /.

Revisit the paragraph that you wrote about your hometown in Lesson 1 / Day 7. Rewrite it below.
☐ ☐ **Practice reading it two times. Focus on stretching the final words of each thought group.**

_____

_____

_____

_____

_____

_____

_____

☐ **Speaking Practice:** Tell someone you know about your hometown (or look in the mirror and tell yourself). As you speak, do not forget to stretch the word endings at the ends of each thought group.

Practice Time Today:	Hrs	Min	Practice Time this Week:	Hrs	Min	Goal for the Week: 3 Hrs

For audio, go to www.myovient.com and enter the audio code shown at the top of this page.

Stretching Practice Audio #80100

The following paragraph has many words ending in "s." This is a sound that many nonnative speakers fail to pronounce clearly. After you stretch the final vowel in each thought group, remember to also add the final "s" sounds at the ends of the phrases.

☐ ☐ ☐ **Read the paragraph three times. Remember to exaggerate your stretching.**

When vacatione—r**s**

snap photo—**s**

for their scrapboo—k**s**,

they don't usually worry about lense—**s**,

flashe—**s**,

or even the people's pose—**s**.

They just "point and cli—ck."

This sty—le

produces photo—**s**

that are grea—t

for uploadi—ng

to social networking si—te**s**,

but without tripo—d**s**,

special lense—**s**

and an eye for bala—n**ce**,

these photo—**s**

will definitely not become screen save—r**s**.

Your family's pose—**s**

in Times Squa—re

probably look just li—ke

your friends' photo—**s**.

Professional photographe—r**s**

always look for sce—ne**s**

and pose—**s**

that are uni—que.

When professiona—l**s**

shoot a photo—,

they pay attentio—n

to the li—ght,

bala—nce,

and messa—ge

that the image gi—ve**s**.

With advances in camera—**s**,

everyday photographe—r**s**

can improve their image—**s**,

but technology alo—ne

will not turn the hobbyi—st**s**

into professiona—l**s**.

To make that ju—mp,

amateu—r**s**

need lesso—n**s**,

not better camera—**s**.

Do not pronounce the second "e" in "scenes." You will learn the reason in Lesson 10.

Practice Time Today:	Hrs	Min	Practice Time this Week:	Hrs	Min	Goal for the Week: 3 Hrs

Stretching Practice Audio #80110

Complete ☐

Read each word and stretch the final vowel sound. Record yourself and listen to your recording. Can you clearly hear the stretching? If not, practice and record yourself again.

☐ ☐ ☐ resea—rch   ☐ ☐ ☐ fu—nds   ☐ ☐ ☐ go—es

☐ ☐ ☐ go—   ☐ ☐ ☐ wi—th   ☐ ☐ ☐ fo—r

☐ ☐ ☐ sou—rce   ☐ ☐ ☐ pla—ns   ☐ ☐ ☐ pla—ce

☐ ☐ ☐ ca—n   ☐ ☐ ☐ openi—ng   ☐ ☐ ☐ tea—m

Write down words that you frequently use at work. Practice stretching these words.

☐ ☐ ☐ _____   ☐ ☐ ☐ _____   ☐ ☐ ☐ _____

☐ ☐ ☐ _____   ☐ ☐ ☐ _____   ☐ ☐ ☐ _____

☐ ☐ ☐ _____   ☐ ☐ ☐ _____   ☐ ☐ ☐ _____

Read each sentence or phrase and stretch the final vowel sound.

☐ ☐ ☐ We got the fu—nds.   ☐ ☐ ☐ Learn the basi—cs.

☐ ☐ ☐ Where she we—nt   ☐ ☐ ☐ Take i—t.

☐ ☐ ☐ What do you crea—te?   ☐ ☐ ☐ Just a—sk.

☐ ☐ ☐ What's the plan of atta—ck?   ☐ ☐ ☐ It was the best advertiseme—nt.

☐ ☐ ☐ I'll be ba—ck.   ☐ ☐ ☐ They built an a—pp.

☐ ☐ ☐ I just reali—zed   ☐ ☐ ☐ It's in the ba—g.

Write down short sentences that you frequently use at work. Practice stretching the last word.

☐ ☐ ☐ _____   ☐ ☐ ☐ _____

☐ ☐ ☐ _____   ☐ ☐ ☐ _____

☐ ☐ ☐ _____   ☐ ☐ ☐ _____

Practice Time Today: ___ Hrs ___ Min   **Practice Time this Week:** ___ Hrs ___ Min   **Goal for the Week: 3 Hrs**

    For audio, go to www.myovient.com and enter the audio code shown at the top of this page.

Stretching Practice Audio #80120

Complete

Look at these self-introductions and mark the thought groups with a slash (/). Read each introduction twice. Practice pausing and stretching the ends of each thought group.

☐ ☐ My name is Keiko Tanaka. I am a marketing specialist at Go-Go Social. I'm a Bay Area native, but I did live in London for 10 years after college. I enjoy cycling and reading about science.

☐ ☐ My name is Maggie Lim. I am a software engineer at a company in Sunnyvale. I speak Chinese, Japanese, and English. I grew up in Singapore, but now I live in Palo Alto. I don't have any hobbies because I seem to be always working.

☐ ☐ My name is Mike Stewart. I am a restaurant blogger. I grew up in Iowa and now live in San Francisco. As you can imagine, I love food. I love eating it, cooking it, and talking about it.

Revisit the self-introduction that you prepared in Lesson 1 / Practice Day 4. Write it again here.
☐ ☐ **Practice reading it two times. Focus on stretching the final words of each thought group.**

_____

_____

_____

_____

_____

_____

☐ **Speaking Practice:** Give your self-introduction to a friend (or in front of a mirror). Do not read it. Instead, try to say it from memory.

Practice Time Today:	Hrs	Min	Practice Time this Week:	Hrs	Min	Goal for the Week: 3 Hrs

Stretching Practice Audio #80130

Complete

Read this story aloud and focus on stretching the sounds at the end of each thought group. Since there are no dashes (—), you will have to decide which sounds to stretch on your own. Many of these words end in "d", so remember to stretch the vowel before the "d". (Some of these thought groups are longer than the thought groups in your previous practice.) Remember to exaggerate your stretching.

☐ ☐ ☐ **Read it three times.**

Enid was an engineer

noted for her research

in computer network security systems.

Although she often analyzed

complicated attacks on computers,

the security system for her house

baffled her.

When she first installed

her own alarm system,

she avoided turning it on

because it beeped

at regular intervals

and bothered her.

She believed

that a system wasn't needed

for her house.

She felt that her neighborhood

was safe.

But after hearing that a thief

had climbed through a neighbor's back window

and robbed him of $500,

she finally asked a technician

for help.

An alarm system rep

visited her house

and realized that Enid had bought

such a complicated system

that it was nearly impossible

to use every day.

He changed some settings

and customized her system

so that it could be controlled

from her computer.

She cheered at that news

because she felt more comfortable

using her computer

than the control box

that had been installed

in her home.

After the tech fixed it,

she thanked him

and offered to give him

a free security upgrade

for his computer.

He declined

because he claimed

he didn't need computer security.

She was astonished

but understood.

She used to think that same thing about her home security!

☐ **Extra Practice:** Talk about your opinion of home or computer security. As you speak, practice stretching your words. Record yourself and listen to the recording.

| Practice Time Today: | Hrs | Min | Practice Time this Week: | Hrs | Min | Goal for the Week: 3 Hrs |

For audio, go to www.myovient.com and enter the audio code shown at the top of this page.

Stretching Practice

Find a book, magazine or article on the Internet and choose one paragraph and read it aloud. Make sure it is something that you have never read before.

☐ ☐ ☐ ☐ ☐ ☐ **Read the paragraph several times. Pay close attention to your stretching. Reading aloud is a great way to practice. We recommend that you read something aloud every day while focusing on one skill (pausing, stretching, etc.) that you are trying to improve.**

Pausing Review

☐ Read the paragraph from your article one more time. This time, pay close attention to your pausing. Make sure you are adding pauses after each thought group.

Self-Reflection:

Write your thoughts about pausing and stretching. Do you feel that you have been able to add pausing and stretching to your speech? Have you received any feedback about your pronunciation since you started practicing pausing and stretching in your daily conversations? What do you need to continue to improve?

_____

_____

_____

_____

_____

_____

_____

_____

Practice Time Today:	Hrs	Min	Practice Time this Week:	Hrs	Min	Goal for the Week: 3 Hrs

Connecting

Complete ☐

What Is Connecting?
Connecting means holding the sound at the end of one word and attaching it to the beginning of the next word. It is also known as blending or linking.

Why Is Connecting Important?
Connecting words is important for maintaining the natural rhythm of English. Native speakers do not read every word in isolation. Instead, they connect words together to make a smooth sound, like a wave.

Incorrect: Native   speakers   don't   read   every   word   in   isolation.

Correct: Nativespeakers   don'treadeveryword   inisolation.

How Should I Connect My Words?
To connect your words, keep your lips, tongue, and mouth in the same position after you finish saying a word. Continue to vocalize that ending sound as you begin the next word. The key is to not stop the sound. If you release the sound, you will sound "choppy." If you hold the sound, your speech will sound smooth. Put your hand on your throat to test whether or not you are connecting your sounds between words. You should feel a constant vibration.

What Words Can I Connect?
You can connect any words together. Some sounds will be easier to connect than others. There are rules for connecting certain sounds, but do not worry about the rules at this point. Just think about connecting everything inside your thought groups.

Can I Use Connecting to Speed Up My Speech?
Yes. When you want to talk quickly but still be understood, you will need to connect sounds inside your thought groups. The sentence below has (at least) three thought groups:

You and Dave   have a meeting at five   in the Aptos office.

To speak quickly, you should connect the words inside the thought groups.

You-wanDave   hava meetin-gat five   in th-yapto-soffice.

Will Connecting Make My Pronunciation Sound Less Clear? No.
Native speakers do not listen for individual sounds or words. Instead, they listen to the rhythm of your speech. Connecting words together will help your rhythm sound more natural.

As you change your speech and try things like connecting, your speech will feel strange. If it feels strange, you are doing it correctly!

REVIEW
Answer these questions without looking at the notes on the left.

What is connecting?

Why is it important?

How do I connect?

Where do I connect?

Can I use connecting to speed up my speech?

Will connecting make my pronunciation sound less clear?

Goal for the Week: 3 Hrs

Connecting Awareness Audio #80140   **Complete** ☐

Read the following phrases and connect all the underlined sounds. Read each one three times.

☐ ☐ ☐   trust is earned   ☐ ☐ ☐   tow away

☐ ☐ ☐   try out   ☐ ☐ ☐   end to end

☐ ☐ ☐   help desk   ☐ ☐ ☐   not yet

☐ ☐ ☐   research and development   ☐ ☐ ☐   lay over

☐ ☐ ☐   big game   ☐ ☐ ☐   competitive environment

☐ ☐ ☐   look old   ☐ ☐ ☐   demand growth

☐ ☐ ☐   knew of him   ☐ ☐ ☐   unique approach

☐ ☐ ☐   save energy   ☐ ☐ ☐   new infrastructure

☐ ☐ ☐   last year   ☐ ☐ ☐   sit down

Read the following sentences and try to connect all of the word endings to the beginning sounds of the next word. (Tip: Keep your voice strong as you move from one word to the next.) Read each one three times.

☐ ☐ ☐   The company had to change the way it did business.

☐ ☐ ☐   The company opted to deploy a new infrastructure.

☐ ☐ ☐   Because customers don't have to pay an annual fee, membership is way up.

☐ ☐ ☐   Although he knew it was illegal, he occasionally parked in a tow away zone.

☐ ☐ ☐   They had a powwow to see if they could finally agree on a new advisor.

Finish these sentences and connect the sounds as you speak. Repeat each sentence three times.

☐ ☐ ☐   We had to....   ☐ ☐ ☐   The problem…

☐ ☐ ☐   It's important that we…   ☐ ☐ ☐   He said that…

☐ ☐ ☐   They wanted us to…   ☐ ☐ ☐   Please…

☐ ☐ ☐   Is there any way that you could…   ☐ ☐ ☐   I think…

☐ ☐ ☐   Would it be possible to…   ☐ ☐ ☐   I don't think…

Practice Time Today:	Hrs	Min	Practice Time this Week:	Hrs	Min	Goal for the Week: 3 Hrs

Connecting   Complete ☐

Write down phrases that you often use at home or work. Practice connecting the words in the phrases. Practice each phrase three times.

☐☐☐ _____   ☐☐☐ _____

☐☐☐ _____   ☐☐☐ _____

☐☐☐ _____   ☐☐☐ _____

☐☐☐ _____   ☐☐☐ _____

☐☐☐ _____   ☐☐☐ _____

Choose ten two-word phrases from a corporate website. (If possible, use your company's website in order to practice words used in your industry.) Write the phrases below. Practice pronouncing the phrases and connecting the words. Practice each phrase three times.

☐☐☐ _____   ☐☐☐ _____

☐☐☐ _____   ☐☐☐ _____

☐☐☐ _____   ☐☐☐ _____

☐☐☐ _____   ☐☐☐ _____

☐☐☐ _____   ☐☐☐ _____

Write three sentences that you might use at your workplace. Practice connecting the words in the sentences. Practice each one three times.

☐☐☐ _____

☐☐☐ _____

☐☐☐ _____

Write three questions that you might ask at your workplace. Practice connecting the words in the questions. Practice each one three times.

☐☐☐ _____

☐☐☐ _____

☐☐☐ _____

Practice Time Today: Hrs ___ Min ___ **Practice Time this Week:** Hrs ___ Min ___ **Goal for the Week: 3 Hrs**

Connecting and Pausing Audio #80150

Complete

Read these sentences. Pauses have been added. Practice connecting the words between each pause.

☐ ☐ ☐ Last year,   we went to Niagara Falls   on our summer vacation.

☐ ☐ ☐ This unique approach   is one   that we've never seen.

☐ ☐ ☐ If you park your car   in a tow away zone   you're sure to get a ticket.

☐ ☐ ☐ Sometimes,   calling the help desk   isn't helpful at all.

☐ ☐ ☐ It's not healthy   to sit at your desk   all day.

☐ ☐ **Read the following speech twice. Practice connecting the words in each thought group.**

What is your future?/
Will you spend your life/
working for someone else?/
Or,//

are you brave enough/
to start your own business?//

Starting your own business/
requires courage,/
perseverance,/
and optimism.//

Do you have/
what it takes?//

First,/
you need courage./
Without courage, /
you will fail.//

Forget what your friends are doing/
in their high-paid jobs/
Forget that your parents told you/
to find a stable job./
To start your own business,/
you must be strong,/
you must be fearless,/
and you must be brave.//

You need courage.//

Second,/
you must have perseverance.//
When you start your business,/
you will have problems./
You will face challenges./
You will want to quit./
Don't!//

To be successful,/
you must persevere.//

Finally,/
you must be optimistic.//

Don't think about failure./
Instead,/
focus on success.//

When you make mistakes,/
learn from them./
When something you try doesn't work,/
think about how you can fix it,/
then move on.//

Optimists find opportunities.//

So,/
do you have it?//

Are you courageous?//

Will you persevere?//

Can you remain optimistic/
in the face of adversity?//

Shhhh,/
don't answer.//

Instead,/
go start your business!//

| Practice Time Today: | Hrs | Min | Practice Time this Week: | Hrs | Min | Goal for the Week: 3 Hrs |

Connecting and Pausing Audio #80160　　　　　　　　　　Complete ☐

Review the pausing rules you studied in Lesson 1. Add connections to the words between the pauses (within the thought groups). Practice each sentence three times.

☐ ☐ ☐　You can join us / on Friday / if you want.

☐ ☐ ☐　You can join us on Friday / if you want.

☐ ☐ ☐　If you don't back up your computer, / you may find yourself / in a terrible situation.

☐ ☐ ☐　If you don't back up your computer, / you may find yourself in a terrible situation.

☐ ☐ ☐　They said the meeting / is rescheduled / for Monday.

☐ ☐ ☐　They said the meeting / is rescheduled for Monday.

☐ ☐ ☐　They said the meeting is rescheduled / for Monday.

☐ ☐ ☐　Francis thought / her invention / would change the world.

☐ ☐ ☐　Francis thought / her invention would change the world.

☐ ☐ ☐　Francis thought her invention / would change the world.

☐ ☐ ☐　The warning signal / is a blinking light / on the dashboard.

☐ ☐ ☐　The warning signal / is a blinking light on the dashboard.

☐ ☐ ☐　The warning signal is a blinking light / on the dashboard.

Write ONE sentence three times. On each line, change the thought groups. Practice reading the sentences. Connect the words within each thought group.

☐ ☐ ☐ _____

☐ ☐ ☐ _____

☐ ☐ ☐ _____

Practice Time Today: ___ Hrs ___ Min　**Practice Time this Week:** ___ Hrs ___ Min　**Goal for the Week: 3 Hrs**

Connecting and Stretching Audio #80170   Complete ☐

Read the following sentences and practice stretching the sounds before the dashes (—). At the same time, connect the sounds that are underlined. Read each sentence three times.

☐ ☐ ☐ Silicon Valley— / is in the southern pa—rt / of the San Francisco Bay Area— / in Northern California—.

☐ ☐ ☐ The term originally refe—rred / to the region's large numbe—r / of silicon chip innovato—rs / and manufacture—rs /, but eventually came to refe—r / to all the high-tech businesse—s / in the area—.

☐ ☐ ☐ Despite the developme—nt / of other high-tech economic cente—rs / throughout the United Sta—tes /, Silicon Valley— / continues to be— / the leading high-tech cente—r / because of its large numbe—r / of enginee—rs / and venture capitali—sts.

The sentences have been copied below without the marks for stretching and connecting. Try to add stretching and connecting naturally. Record yourself and listen to the recording. Can you clearly hear the rhythm of English in your voice?

Silicon Valley is in the southern part of the San Francisco Bay Area in Northern California. The term originally referred to the region's large number of silicon chip innovators and manufacturers but eventually came to refer to all the high-tech businesses in the area. Despite the development of other high-tech economic centers throughout the United States, Silicon Valley continues to be the leading high-tech center because of its large number of engineers and venture capitalists.

When you add stretching and connecting to your speech, your speech should feel smooth. Your voice should flow gently like a wave. It should feel like you are lengthening your voice, and you should sound very calm when you are speaking.

| Practice Time Today: | Hrs | Min | **Practice Time this Week:** | Hrs | Min | **Goal for the Week: 3 Hrs** |

Connecting and Stretching Audio #80180   Complete ☐

**Read the speech below from Lesson 2. As you read it, make sure you stretch
the vowels at the ends of each thought group. At the same time, practice
connecting the words inside the thought groups.** ☐ ☐ **Read it two times.**

When vacationers snap photos for their scrapbooks, they don't
usually worry about lenses, flashes, or even the people's poses. They just "point
and click." This style produces photos that are great for uploading to social
networking sites, but without tripods, special lenses and an eye for balance, these
photos will definitely not become screen savers. Your family's poses in Times
Square probably look just like your friends' photos. Professional photographers
always look for scenes and poses that are unique. When professionals shoot a
photo, they pay attention to the light, balance, and message that the image gives.
With advances in cameras, everyday photographers can improve their images, but
technology alone will not turn the hobbyists into professionals. To make that jump,
amateurs need lessons, not better cameras.

☐ **Write a paragraph about your own experiences with photography. Read it aloud and practice
pausing, stretching and connecting.**

_____

_____

_____

_____

_____

_____

_____

*If you ask native English speakers if they connect words
together, they might tell you that they do not. Most people do
not realize that they do this because it happens quickly.*

Practice Time Today: ___ Hrs ___ Min **Practice Time this Week:** ___ Hrs ___ Min **Goal for the Week: 3 Hrs**

          For audio, go to www.myovient.com and enter the audio code shown at the top of this page.

Putting It All Together (Pause, Stretch, Connect)

Complete ☐

Think about your job. What tasks do you do daily? What tasks do you do yearly? What skills do you need in order to do your job well? Write a description of your job below.

_____

_____

_____

_____

_____

_____

_____

Review Activity 1

☐ Draw lines between the thought groups in your paragraph. (Lesson 1)

☐ Read the paragraph and focus on pausing.

☐ Circle the sounds that should be stretched. (Lesson 2)

☐ Read the paragraph and focus on pausing and stretching.

☐ Underline the words that you can connect. (Lesson 3)

☐ Read the paragraph and focus on pausing, stretching, and connecting.

Review Activity 2

☐ Without looking at the paragraph you just practiced, talk about your job. Try to include pausing, stretching, and connecting while you speak. Record yourself and listen to the recording.

Review Activity 3

☐ Talk about your hobbies or interests. As you speak, focus on the three basic elements of pronunciation (pausing, stretching, connecting). Record yourself and listen to the recording.

If you are comfortable with pausing, stretching, and connecting, then you may move on to the next lesson in this book. If you are not confident in your pausing, stretching, or connecting, repeat the first three lessons and spend more time practicing these skills in your daily conversations until you are ready.

| Practice Time Today: | Hrs | Min | **Practice Time this Week:** | Hrs | Min | **Goal for the Week: 3 Hrs** |

STOP

Do not go to the next lesson until you
have mastered the first three lessons!

Part Two of this book focuses on more advanced pronunciation topics: RHYTHM, CONNECTIONS, and SOUNDS. We use the image of stairs to explain the importance of each topic. The first stair step (RHYTHM) is the most important part of pronunciation. RHYTHM affects comprehension the most. In other words, if you learn to speak with the correct American English RHYTHM, native speakers will have an easier time understanding you. You need to start on this step.

The next step, and the next topic you will study, is CONNECTIONS. When you learn how to link, blend, and delete sounds correctly, your speech will sound smoother and more natural.

The final step is SOUNDS. This is the last topic you will study. You will learn tips for improving your individual SOUNDS. We wait until the end of our book to talk about sounds for two reasons: One, it may be difficult to change your pronunciation of a certain sound, causing you to feel frustrated and give up. Two, it is often the least important skill for comprehension. Your listeners can usually guess your meaning from context even if you mispronounce a sound.

Try to master each step, starting at the bottom, before moving up to the next one. Changing your pronunciation is hard work, but if you keep practicing, you will see improvement.

Word Stress

What Is "Word Stress"?
Word stress is a term that describes the extra stress or power that gets placed on a single word in a sentence. (This is sometimes called "sentence stress.") Just like *pausing* and *stretching*, *stress* is one aspect of the rhythm of English.

How Do I Put Stress on a Word?
Stressed words are a little longer (stretched), a little higher pitched, and a little louder than the other words in a sentence.

How Do I Know Which Words to Stress?
Simply put, you should stress the important key words of a sentence. Usually, this means the words that give new information. In the following example, the stressed words are in bold: The **table** is in the **middle** of the **room**.

As you can see, the meaning of the sentence is contained in the bold words. Without these words, the sentence would be "The is in the of the."

When we listen to English, we listen for these stressed words (also known as *content* words). If the unstressed words (*function* words) are just as strong as the stressed words, the rhythm will sound strange. The *content words* should be strong; the *function* words should be soft.

The table is in the middle of the room. = Unnatural

The table **is in the** middle **of the** room. = Unnatural

The **table** is in the **middle** of the **room.** = Natural

What does the Rhythm of English Sound Like?
If you stress only the key words, then your English will sound like a smooth wave or pulse.

> *du du DA du du DA... (soft, soft, strong, soft, soft, strong...)*

If you stress all of the words in a sentence, your sentences will sound too strong or forceful.

> *DA DA DA DA... (strong, strong, strong, strong...)*

Some people say this sounds like a machine gun or a hammer pounding a nail. If you speak like this, your English will sound harsh and may sound rude.

How Can I Practice?
One way to improve your rhythm is to listen to native speakers on the radio, TV, or the Internet. As you listen, repeat the phrases that you hear and mimic the rhythm that you hear. You can also use body movements to feel the rhythm. Remind yourself to make changes by stepping up onto your toes, pushing your hand forward, or lifting your chin while you are practicing.

As you change your speech and try things like word stress, your speech will feel strange. If it feels strange, you are doing it correctly!

REVIEW
Answer these questions without looking at the notes on the left.

What is word stress?

How do I stress a word?

Which words are stressed?

Which words are not stressed?

What does correct rhythm sound like?

How can I practice?

Goal for the Week: 3 Hrs

Word Stress Audio #80190

Complete ☐

☐ **Read and stress the bold words.**

Enid was an **engineer**

noted for her **research**

in **computer** network

security systems.

Although she often **analyzed**

complicated attacks

on **computers**,

the **security** system

for her **house**

baffled her.

When she **first** installed

her own **alarm** system,

she **avoided**

turning it **on**

because it **beeped**

at regular **intervals**

and **bothered** her.

She **believed**

that a **system**

wasn't **needed**

for her **house**.

She felt her **neighborhood**

was **safe**.

You have complete control of where you place your stress. If you want to emphasize a word, simply add more stress to that word.

SOUNDS
CONNECTIONS
RHYTHM

☐ **Think of a few sentence of your own. Break the sentences into phrases. Write one phrase on each line below.**

_____

_____

_____

_____

_____

_____

_____

_____

_____

_____

_____

_____

_____

Did you notice that every thought group had at least one stressed word?

| Practice Time Today: | Hrs | Min | **Practice Time this Week:** | Hrs | Min | **Goal for the Week: 3 Hrs** |

Word Stress (Compound Nouns) Audio #80200   Complete

A compound noun is a noun made up of two or more words. The first word of a compound noun is usually stressed.

greenhouse (a glass building where plants grow)

SOUNDS
CONNECTIONS
RHYTHM

When you use an adjective and a noun that do not form a compound noun, the noun is stressed.

green **house** (a house that is green)

Stress the first word of these compound nouns:

☐ ☐ ☐ **office** system   ☐ ☐ ☐ **conference** call

☐ ☐ ☐ **project** manager   ☐ ☐ ☐ **product** manager

☐ ☐ ☐ **business** person   ☐ ☐ ☐ **business** community

☐ ☐ ☐ **business** strategy   ☐ ☐ ☐ **marketing** strategy

☐ ☐ ☐ **sales** call   ☐ ☐ ☐ **sales** team

☐ ☐ ☐ **mailing** list   ☐ ☐ ☐ **flash** drive

☐ ☐ ☐ **account** balance   ☐ ☐ ☐ **board** meeting

☐ ☐ ☐ **White** House   ☐ ☐ ☐ **security** system

Stress the first part of these compound nouns.

☐ ☐ ☐ **fund**raiser   ☐ ☐ ☐ **soft**ware   ☐ ☐ ☐ **net**work

☐ ☐ ☐ **key**board   ☐ ☐ ☐ **chair**person ☐ ☐ ☐ **board**room

☐ ☐ ☐ **head**line   ☐ ☐ ☐ **whole**sale   ☐ ☐ ☐ **feed**back

☐ ☐ ☐ **week**end   ☐ ☐ ☐ **over**head   ☐ ☐ ☐ **dead**lock

☐ ☐ ☐ **dead**line   ☐ ☐ ☐ **up**date   ☐ ☐ ☐ **hand**shake

☐ **Create some sentences using a few of the words on this page. Read them aloud and practice adding word stress.**

Practice Time Today: ___ Hrs ___ Min **Practice Time this Week:** ___ Hrs ___ Min **Goal for the Week: 3 Hrs**

Word Stress Audio #80210

Complete

Read these two paragraphs aloud and stress the words that are in bold. Record yourself and listen to your recording to see if you can hear the stressed words clearly.

SOUNDS
CONNECTIONS
RHYTHM

☐ **Paragraph 1**

Most of today's customer **service** is done on the **telephone** or the **Web**. Companies use **operators, touch**-tone automated services, and **call**-centers to meet the customers' **needs** in an attempt to save **money. Similarly,** a lot of companies **encourage** customers to go **online** to have their questions and issues **answered** via **chat, FAQ,** virtual **agent,** or **email.** However, even though these are cost-effective **measures,** customers **often** miss the old-**fashioned** method of face-to-face **service.**

☐ **Paragraph 2**

Most of **today's** customer **service** is done on the **telephone** or the **Web.** Companies use **operators, touch**-tone automated services, and **call**-centers to meet the customers' **needs** in an **attempt** to save **money. Similarly,** a lot of companies encourage **customers** to go **online** to have their **questions** and **issues** answered via **chat, FAQ,** virtual **agent,** or **email. However,** even though these **are** cost-effective **measures,** customers often **miss** the old-**fashioned** method of **face-to-face** service.

1. Which paragraph makes it sound like the new ways of providing customer service are good?

2. Which paragraph makes it sound like the new ways of providing customer service are NOT good?

Answers

1. The speaker in paragraph 1 feels that the new ways of providing customer service are good. The speaker stresses positive words like customer, encourage, and service. The speaker emphasizes that customers get the answers they want via online help.

2. The speaker in paragraph 2 feels that the new ways of providing customer service are not good. The speaker stresses negative words like attempt, customers, and miss. The speaker emphasizes that companies are saving money while customers have to work harder to get the answers they want.

Word Stress (Stress and Meaning) Audio #80220

Complete

☐ **Read the following sentences and stress the bold words. Notice that the meaning changes depending on which word you are stressing.**

SOUNDS
CONNECTIONS
RHYTHM

Statement		Reply
1. a. I can **ski.**	→	You must like cold weather.
b. I can ski **tomorrow.**	→	Good. Let's meet at 8 AM.
2. a. I can **go.**	→	Good. I'm looking forward to it.
b. I **can't** go.	→	I wish you could.
3. a. He can call **anytime.**	→	Great. He might call at noon.
b. He can **call** anytime .	→	OK. I'll tell him not to email but to call you.
4. a. Can you **read** this?	→	Yes, it says "Do not enter!" in French.
b. Can you read **this?**	→	Yes, I can read this one but not the other one.
5. a. I can **do** it	→	I knew you could!
b. I **can't** do it.	→	Try again.
6. a. She can sing **well.**	→	Yes, she has three gold records.
b. She can **sing** well.	→	You're right, but she can't play the guitar at all.

☐ **Write your own sentences and change where you put the stress. Write a reply that you might hear.**

_____ → _____

_____ → _____

_____ → _____

_____ → _____

☐ **Listen to a news reporter on TV or the radio. Write two sentences that you hear. Circle the words that are stressed.**

1. _____

_____

2. _____

_____

Practice Time Today: Hrs Min **Practice Time this Week:** Hrs Min **Goal for the Week: 3 Hrs**

For audio, go to www.myovient.com and enter the audio code shown at the top of this page.

Word Stress (Poetry and Music) Audio #80230   Complete ☐

Poets and song writers often use the rhythm of English in their work. We do not always speak this way, but practicing the rhythm of poetry and music can help you feel the rhythm of English.

☐ **Read these poems and stress the bold words.**

Bob the Developer:

There **once** was a de**vel**oper named **Bob**,
who **could**n't find **joy** in his **job**.
He **want**ed to **quit**, but he **could**n't ad**mit**
that he **did** love to **hear** himself **sob**.

An office poem:

The **lights** are not **on** –
not a **soul** to be **found**.
The **boss** must be **gone**
'cause **no** one's **around**.

☐ **Find a song or poem and write some of it here. Which words are stressed? Circle the stressed words. Practice reading or singing it. If you choose a song, try singing it along with the artist and see if you can stress the same words.**

_____

_____

_____

_____

_____

_____

_____

Practice Time Today:	Hrs	Min	Practice Time this Week:	Hrs	Min	Goal for the Week: 3 Hrs

Word Stress Audio #80240   Complete

☐ **Read this paragraph and practice stressing the bold words.**

SOUNDS
CONNECTIONS
RHYTHM

When **vacationers** snap photos for their **scrapbooks**, they don't usually worry about **lenses, flashes**, or even the people's **poses**. They just "**point** and **click**." This style produces **photos** that are **great** for uploading to social **networking** sites, but without **tripods**, special **lenses** and an eye for **balance**, these photos will definitely **not** become **screen** savers. Your family's poses in Times **Square** probably look just like your **friends'** photos. **Professional** photographers always look for **scenes** and **poses** that are **unique**. When **professionals** shoot a **photo**, they pay **attention** to the **light**, **balance**, and **message** that the image **gives**. With advances in **cameras**, **everyday** photographers can improve their **images**, but technology **alone** will not turn the **hobbyists** into **professionals**. To make **that** jump, amateurs need **lessons**, not better **cameras**.

☐ **Read this paragraph again, but this time, do not read the words. Instead, try to hum the rhythm. (Make a sound with your voice, but keep your mouth closed.) You should hum more loudly on the stressed words.**

☐ **Read this paragraph again, but this time, as you read, stretch a rubber band as you pronounce the stressed words.**

☐ **Read this paragraph again, but this time, stand up while you read. Every time you read a stressed word, raise yourself up on your toes.**

☐ **Finally, summarize this paragraph without looking at the words. Do your best to include correct word stress.**

| Practice Time Today: | Hrs | Min | **Practice Time this Week:** | Hrs | Min | **Goal for the Week: 3 Hrs** |

For audio, go to www.myovient.com and enter the audio code shown at the top of this page.

Word Stress Review Audio #80250

Complete ☐

☐ **Circle the words in each sentence that should be stressed. Read the sentence and add extra stress on those words.**

SOUNDS
CONNECTIONS
RHYTHM

How have you been?   I couldn't agree more.

I agree with you 100 percent.   His speech was fabulous.

It's not the way that he looks, but the way that he talks that's impressive.

☐ **Listen to a short recording of someone reading the news. As you listen, repeat what the person says right after he says it. Try to speak at the same pace as the speaker. (This is called "shadowing.")**

Self-Reflection:

Write your feelings about your pronunciation improvement so far. Have you had any positive feedback this week from your friends or coworkers?

_____

_____

_____

_____

_____

_____

_____

_____

_____

Practice Time Today:	Hrs	Min	**Practice Time this Week:**	Hrs	Min	**Goal for the Week: 3 Hrs**

Intonation

What Is "Intonation"?

Intonation is the rising and falling of the pitch of your voice. It is part of the rhythm of English. It helps to think of intonation like the notes on a musical scale. Just as notes can go up and down, you can use intonation to make your voice go up and down. You can also think of intonation as steps going up or down or as a wave that moves up and down like the ocean. Just remember that when you speak English, your voice should not be flat. It should be moving.

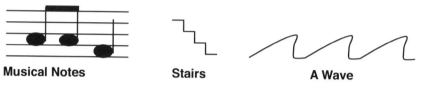

Musical Notes   **Stairs**   **A Wave**

Where Do I Add Intonation in My Speech?

Intonation follows the patterns of word stress. When you stress a word, you should also raise the pitch of your voice. The stronger you stress a word, the higher your pitch should be. The line over this sentence shows how your voice should move up and down as you say this sentence.

There was a **fire** on the corner of **First** and **Main** Streets last **night**.

What Does a Rising Intonation Indicate?

Rising intonation at the end of a sentence means that you are asking a question that requires a *yes* or *no* answer, or that you are unsure of your statement.

What Does a Falling Intonation Indicate?

Falling intonation at the end of a sentence means that you have made a statement that you are confident is true. The more your voice falls, the stronger the statement. In addition, questions that ask *who, what, where, when,* & *how* end in a falling intonation pattern.

How Can I Practice Intonation?

If you have trouble adding intonation to your voice, try these tips:

Stand up. Move onto your toes when you want your intonation to go up. Then move back onto flat feet when you are lowering your intonation.

Look in the mirror. When you want your intonation to go up, lift your chin. Then move your chin down as you lower your intonation.

Record yourself. Listen to your own speech and practice changing your intonation. Record yourself talking freely as well as reading from a text.

Shadow other speakers. Play different types of audio (news shows, dramas, commercials, interviews), and practice intonation by repeating what you hear. Try to repeat as fast as you can for as long as you can. It is okay to skip words you cannot understand.

REVIEW
Answer these questions without looking at the notes on the left.

What is intonation?

Where do I add intonation in my speech?

What does a rising intonation indicate?

What does a falling intonation indicate?

How can I practice?

Goal for the Week: 3 Hrs

For audio, go to www.myovient.com and enter the audio code shown at the top of this page.

Intonation

The Secret to American English Intonation

When Americans speak in English, they naturally raise the pitch of their voices to a pitch that is higher than their relaxed voice. If they spoke in a natural relaxed pitch, their voices would sound quite low. Many languages utilize this relaxed, low pitch without modification. In English, however, speakers modify their pitch by raising it a few notes higher than their relaxed voice.

Natural Pitch:

Raised Pitch (American English):

Raising the pitch of your voice will make it much easier for you to add intonation to your speech. If you speak using a relaxed, low pitch, it will be very difficult to add falling intonation because your voice will already be at the bottom of its range. There will be no room for your voice to "fall."

Voice Range

However, if you raise the pitch of your voice, you will have a lot of room to add both rising and falling intonation:

Voice Range

When you are practicing your English pronunciation, think of the levels **3**, **2**, and **1**. Level 3 is a high pitch. Use this when emphasizing words. Level 2 is a medium pitch. Use this for most of the words in your sentences. Level 1 is a low pitch. Use this at the ends of your statements. These are relative levels; one person's 3 might be another person's 2.

Play around with your personal pitch range. Practice going up to level 3 and then down to level 1.

Note: If you are male, you might wonder if raising your pitch will make you sound like a female. You should not worry. You only need to raise your pitch slightly so that you are able to bring it down at the ends of phrases and sentences.

Intonation Audio #80260

Complete

Before studying the rules of intonation, you should try a few activities to practice changing the intonation (pitch) of your voice.

SOUNDS
CONNECTIONS
RHYTHM

☐ **Practice your intonation by making your voice go up and down with the arrows.**

mmmmm MM mmmmm MM mmmmm MM mmmmm MM mm

mmmmm MM mmmmm MM mmmmm MM mmmmm MM

du du du DA du du du DA du du du DA du du du DA du

du du du DA du du du DA du du du DA du du du DA

☐ **Use rising intonation when you say these words:**

Hello?   Really?   Ready?   Now?   Excuse me?

☐ **Use falling intonation when you say these words:**

Hello.   Really.   Ready.   Now.   Excuse me.

☐ **Read these sentences and make your voice go up and down where the words go up and down.**

I like their business model.   I'll be there at five.

He got promoted last year.   She's going to call at nine.

☐ **Make your own sentences and mark the intonation.**

_____

_____

_____

_____

For audio, go to www.myovient.com and enter the audio code shown at the top of this page.

Intonation Audio #80270   Complete ☐

☐ **Practice adding intonation to your voice while reading this dialog between a receptionist and a visitor.**

Follow the lines and arrows with your voice. The top line is intonation level 3. The middle line is intonation level 2, and the bottom line is intonation level 1.

Receptionist:	How can I help you?
Visitor:	I'm here to see Tom Holtz.
Receptionist:	Do you have an appointment with him?
Visitor:	Yes. At 3:30. I'm a little early.
Receptionist:	OK. I'll let him know that you're here. Could you please sign in?
Visitor:	Sure.
Receptionist:	If you'd like something to drink, we've got coffee and tea over there.
Visitor:	Thanks. Do you have water?
Receptionist:	Of course, there's a water dispenser next to the coffee.
Visitor::	Thanks.

☐ **Record yourself reading this dialog and listen to the recording. Can you hear your intonation? Does the pitch of your voice correctly follow the line pattern?**

☐ **Write your own dialog. Add intonation lines and arrows above your sentences. Practice reading your dialog.**

Intonation (Questions) Audio #80280

Complete

Read and practice these intonation rules.

1. ☐ **Yes/No Questions:** a) Questions that ask for a *yes* or *no* answer require a strong *rising* intonation on the stressed words and on the final word of the sentence. b) When you want to ask a quick question or one that is not very important, keep your pitch flatter. (Do not go all the way to level 3.)

1-a) Do you take the **train** to **work**?

1-b) Do you take the **train** to work?

Do you like your **commute?**

Do you like your **commute?**

2. ☐ **Tag Questions:** a) To confirm a statement, *raise* your intonation on the stressed word and then *let it fall*. Then, *raise* your intonation again on the question tag. b) *Falling* intonation on the tag implies that you think you know the answer, and you want the listener to agree with you.

2-a) You take the **train** to **work,** right?

2-b) You take the **train** to **work, don't** you?

It's really **nice** outside, isn't **it**?

It's really **nice** outside, isn't **it**?

3. ☐ **Information Questions:** a) Questions that ask for information require a *rising* and *falling* intonation on the stressed word at the end of the question. b) If the stressed word is not the last word of the sentence, then the intonation *rises* on the stressed word and then *falls* on the final word(s).

3-a) How long is your **commute?**

3-b) How long does it take you to get to **work** every day?

What is your **name?**

What's your **last** name?

Continued on next page

For audio, go to www.myovient.com and enter the audio code shown at the top of this page.

Intonation (Questions) Audio #80280 **Complete** ☐

4. ☐ **Questions with a Choice: a)** Questions that ask you to make a choice have *rising* intonation on the first choice and *falling* intonation on the second choice. **b)** If the question has more than two choices, the intonation *rises* on all the choices except the final one. The final choice has *falling* intonation. **c)** The intonation *rises* on all choices if the speaker wants to indicate that there may be more choices or that the listener does not have to make a choice at all.

4-a) Do you want **coffee** or **tea?**　　　*4-b)* Do you want **coffee, tea,** or **soda?**

4-c) Do you want **coffee** or **tea?** *(You do not have to choose either one.)*

5. ☐ **Statements into Questions** You can turn a statement into a question by adding *rising* intonation on the stressed words at the end of the sentence. This can be used to show surprise.

5) You left at **five** in the **morning?**

Intonation (Questions) Audio #80290

Complete

☐ **Read the following questions aloud. Decide if each question has a rising or falling intonation pattern. Draw an arrow over the word that has the intonation. The answers are below in the box.**

1. Are you an owner or employee?

2. How many people work in your office?

3. Do you have what it takes to be successful?

4. Your name is Kate, isn't it? (You are pretty sure her name is Kate.)

5. Do you have a Korean or a Japanese car? (This is **not** an "either/or" question.)

6. How many years have you worked for this company?

7. Who called?

8. That company got $3 million in funding?! (You are surprised.)

Possible Answers

1. Rise on *owner,* Fall on *employee*
2. Rise/Fall on *office*
3. Rise on *have, takes,* & *successful*
4. Rise/Fall on *Kate*; Rise on *isn't*, Fall on *it*
5. Rise on *Korean*; Rise on *Japanese car*
6. Rise/Fall on *company*
7. Rise/Fall on *called*
8. Rise on *funding*

☐ **Write down three work-related questions you might ask a colleague, and then draw arrows indicating the pattern of intonation for each question.**

1. _____

_____

2. _____

_____

3. _____

_____

Practice Time Today: Hrs   Min   **Practice Time this Week:**   Hrs   Min   **Goal for the Week: 3 Hrs**

Intonation (Statements) Audio #80300

Complete ☐

Read and practice these intonation rules.

1. ☐ **General Statements** a) Just like informational questions, statements require a rising and falling pitch on the final stressed word of each phrase. b) If the stressed word is not the last word, then the pitch rises on the stressed word and falls on the final word of the sentence.

*1-a) I need to call him **tomorrow**.*

*I need to call him **tomorrow** at the **latest**.*

*1-b) Sorry to **interrupt** you.*

*Let me **talk** to him.*

2. ☐ **Series** a) Statements that list a series of words have a rising pitch on each word in the series and falling pitch on the final word. b) In a list that is not finished (an "open" series), the pitch rises on every item in the series. (This indicates there are more options.)

2-a) We're meeting the CEO, CFO and the COO.

I called, faxed, and emailed him.

2-b) My hobbies are running, surfing, skiing...

We need to talk to James, Beth, Paul...

3. ☐ **Introductory Words and Phrases** a) If you begin your sentence with introductory words, the pitch should rise and fall on the introductory words. b) The introductory words can also have a rise-fall-rise pitch pattern.

3-a) Actually, I'm not going.

On the other hand, it's expensive.

3-b) Actually, I'm not going.

On the other hand, it's expensive.

4. ☐ **Additional Information** If you add additional information to the middle of a sentence, you need to show that it is not part of the main sentence. You do this by flattening the intonation, saying the information quickly, and adding a pause at the beginning and end of the extra phrase.

4) The president, / I think he went to your university, / will be there.

5. ☐ **Sarcasm** You can say the opposite of what you mean by stretching the word that is not true, and by using stretched rising and falling intonation. Keep the rest of the sentence flat.

5) I just l o v e having my performance review.
(You do not really love it.)

He has the f r i e n d l i e s t personality.
(He is not friendly.)

| Practice Time Today: | Hrs | Min | **Practice Time this Week:** | Hrs | Min | **Goal for the Week: 3 Hrs** |

For audio, go to www.myovient.com and enter the audio code shown at the top of this page.

Intonation Audio #80310   Complete

☐ **Read the following statements aloud. Decide if each statement should have a rising or falling intonation pattern. Draw an arrow over the word that has the intonation. The answers are below in the box.**

SOUNDS
CONNECTIONS
RHYTHM

1. The employees of this company are treated very well.

2. Your commuting options are riding a train, bus or bike.

3. A successful person takes risks every day.

4. This store sells computers, printers, phones, appliances....

5. You can have coffee or tea.

6. I just love going to the dentist. (I really hate it.)

7. The conference room, the one we were in last week, was really cold.

8. Interestingly, they didn't call us back.

Possible Answers

1. Rise/Fall on *employees, company, well*
2. Rise on *commuting*; Fall on *options*; Rise on *train, bus*; Fall on *bike*
3. Rise on *successful*; Fall on *person*; Rise/Fall on *risks*; Rise on *every*; Fall on *day*
4. Rise on *computers, printers, phones, appliances*
5. Rise on *coffee*; Fall on *tea*
6. Stretched **rise/fall** on *love*; Rise/Fall on *dentist*
7. Rise on *conference*; Fall on *room*; Flat pitch on *the one we were in last week*; Fall on *cold*
8. Rise/Fall on *interestingly*; Rise/Fall on *back*

☐ **Think of three suggestions for staying relaxed even when you have a lot of work to do. Write three statements explaining your suggestions. Read your statements, record your voice, and listen to your recording. Can you hear the intonation in your voice?**

1. _____

2. _____

3. _____

| **Practice Time Today:** | Hrs | Min | **Practice Time this Week:** | Hrs | Min | **Goal for the Week: 3 Hrs** |

For audio, go to www.myovient.com and enter the audio code shown at the top of this page.

Intonation Review

Complete

News Reporters

☐ Listen to a news report on TV or on the radio.

☐ Did you notice that news reporters speak with a lot of intonation?

☐ Shadow the speaker and practice following his/her intonation patterns.

☐ Imagine you are a news reporter and record yourself reporting on a story from your own life.

Conversation

☐ Listen to a conversation from a TV show or movie.

☐ Did you notice that casual conversations also use a lot of intonation? Casual conversations often have strong ups and downs.

☐ Shadow one speaker and practice following the intonation patterns.

☐ Imagine you are having a conversation with someone and record yourself speaking.

Inspirational Speech

☐ Find a speech on the Internet by a world leader, politician, business leader, or inspirational speaker who is speaking passionately about a topic and listen to a few minutes of it.

☐ Did you notice that when a speaker is passionate about a topic his intonation has strong ups and downs?

☐ Shadow the speaker and practice following his/her intonation patterns.

☐ Imagine you are giving an inspirational or passionate speech and record yourself speaking.

Think about the intonation used in the situations below. How does the intonation differ when someone is:

☐ Making public announcements?　☐ Selling products on TV?　☐ Reading stories to children?

☐ Screaming in pain ?　☐ Yelling in anger?　☐ Asking for a favor?

☐ **Choose a paragraph from a newspaper or book and practice reading it aloud. Read it three or four times, changing your style of intonation each time.**

| **Practice Time Today:** | Hrs | Min | **Practice Time this Week:** | Hrs | Min | **Goal for the Week: 3 Hrs** |

Syllable Stress

Complete ☐

What Is a Syllable?
A syllable is a unit of sound that includes only <u>one</u> spoken vowel. A syllable can contain consonants, but it does not have to. The word *service* has two syllables because it has two spoken vowels (e, i). The final *e* is silent.

Some people like to think of a syllable as a beat of music. You can feel the "beat" by clapping your hands to the syllables. If you say the word *service,* you would clap once on "ser" and once on "vice" (ser-vice).

What Is Syllable Stress?
Syllable stress is the emphasis we place on one syllable in a word. We create stress by making the syllable a little louder, longer, and higher-pitched. One way to feel the stress on a syllable is to take a rubber band and pull it apart when you are stressing the sound.

You know that the word *service* has two syllables. Which syllable is stressed? The first syllable contains the stress: **SER**-*vice.*

Can I Ever Stress More Than One Syllable in a Word?
Yes. However, words with one, two or three syllables will have only one strongly stressed syllable. Words with four or more syllables will have one syllable with strong (primary) stress and one syllable with medium (secondary) stress. For example, the word *education* has four syllables: *ed-u-ca-tion.* The primary stress is on *CA* and the secondary stress is on *ED* → *ED-u-**CA**-tion.*

What Happens to the Unstressed Syllables?
The unstressed syllables in a word sound weaker and shorter than the stressed syllables. The vowels in the unstressed syllables are usually shortened to "uh" or "eh" sounds and are sometimes completely ignored. For example, the "a" in *about* sounds like "uh" (*uh-bout*).

Will Changing a Word's Syllable Stress Change the Meaning?
Sometimes the meaning of a word will change if a different syllable is stressed. Take the word "object," for example. **OB**ject is a noun that means a material thing that can be touched; ob**JECT** is a verb that means to show your disagreement with something. This often happens with two-syllable nouns and verbs.

Do I Need to Memorize Rules for Syllable Stress?
No, you do not need to worry about memorizing a lot of rules. It is better to memorize the syllable stress for the words that you commonly use. When you learn a new word, you should also memorize the syllable stress for that word.

How Can I Learn Which Syllable to Stress?
The best way to learn which syllable to stress in a word is to look in a dictionary. The stressed syllable is often marked with **bold** lettering, in CAPITAL LETTERS, with an <u>underline</u>, or with a special mark (') in front of the stressed syllable. Check the guide in your dictionary to find out how that dictionary marks stress.

REVIEW
Answer these questions without looking at the notes on the left.

What is a syllable?

What is syllable stress?

Can I stress more than one syllable in a word?

Can changing syllable stress change a word's meaning?

Do I need to memorize syllable stress rules ?

How can I learn which syllable is stressed?

Goal for the Week: 3 Hrs

Syllable Stress Audio #80320   Complete ☐

In Lesson 4, you learned how to add stress to the keywords in a sentence. In this chapter, you will practice adding stress to the syllables inside words. Every word that has two or more syllables has one syllable that is stressed more than the others.

This phrase is written with different sized letters to show you how to stress words and syllables. The bigger the letter, the more stress it has:

When vaCAtioners snap PHOtos for their SCRAPbooks

☐ **Read this paragraph and stress the words and syllables according to the size of the letters. The larger the letters, the more stress you should add. Hold a rubber band as you read the paragraph. Stretch the rubber band whenever you add stress.**

When vaCAtioners snap PHOtos for their SCRAPbooks, they don't USually WOrry about LENses, FLAshes, or Even the PEOple's POSes. They just "POINT and CLICK." This STYle proDUces PHOtos that are GREAT for UPloading to SOcial NETworking sites, but withOUT TRIpods, SPEcial LENses and an eye for BALance, these PHOtos will DEfinitely NOT beCOME SCREEN SAvers. Your FAmily's POses in TImes SQUARE PRObably look just like your FRIENDS' PHOtos. ProFESsional phoTOgraphers ALways look for SCENES and POses that are uNIque. When proFESsionals shoot a PHOto, they pay atTENtion to the LIGHT, BAlance, and MESsage that the Image GIVES. With adVANces in CAMeras, EVeryday phoTOgraphers can imPROVE their Images, but techNOlogy aLONE will not turn the HOBbyists into proFESsionals. To make THAT jump, Amateurs need LESsons, not better CAMeras.

Practice Time Today:	Hrs	Min	Practice Time this Week:	Hrs	Min	Goal for the Week: 3 Hrs

Lesson 6 / Practice Day 2

55

Syllable Stress (Rules) Audio #80330

Complete ☐

SOUNDS
CONNECTIONS
RHYTHM

☐ Read through the list of rules below and practice stressing the correct syllables. These are rules that you can generally apply to English words. Just remember, all English rules have exceptions!

Stress on 1st Syllable

Two-Syllable Nouns: **AC**cess / **AD**dress
Two-Syllable Adjectives: **GOR**geous / **HAP**py
Two-Syllable Adverbs: **PRET**ty / **QUICK**ly / **BAD**ly
Nouns made of two words: **PASS**word / **WHITE**board / **HAND**shake

Stress on 2nd Syllable

Two-Syllable Verbs: ap**PLY** / sug**GEST**
Verbs made of two words: under**STAND** / over**FLOW**

Stress on Words with Prefixes and Suffixes:

Prefixes (a-, un-, be-, in-, pro-, ex-, ob-, dis-, re-) are usually not stressed. The word they attach to keeps its original stress pattern even when a prefix is attached.

- **DO** → un**DO**
- **AC**tivate → re**AC**tivate
- **PROVE** → im**PROVE**

Suffixes sometimes change the stress of a word (-s, -ed, -ing, -ish, -ly, -ee, -ic).

- Stress these suffixes: -eer (**EN**gine → engin**EER**) / -aire (**QUE**stion → questionn**AIRE**)

- Do not stress these suffixes: -less (**EF**fort → **EF**fortless) / -ing (**O**pen → **O**pening) / -er (de**VE**lop → de**VE**loper)

- For words with other suffixes, follow the patterns below:

Stress the syllable second from the end:
[-ic] do-**MES**-tic, geo-**GRA**-phic
[-sion] in-**VA**-sion
[-tion] app-li-**CA**-tion
[-stion] **QUES**-tion
[-ing] a-**MA**-zing

Stress the syllable third from the end:
[-cy] de-**MO**-cra-cy   [-full] **BEAU**-ti-ful
[-phy] pho-**TO**-gra-phy   [-ly] **FRE**-quen-tly
[-ty] pri-**OR**-i-ty   [-ical] tech-no-**LO**-gi-cal
[-gy] the-**O**-lo-gy   [-able] ad-**JUS**-ta-ble
[-al] **CRI**-ti-cal   [-ate] ap-**PRE**-ci-ate

Practice Time Today:	Hrs	Min	Practice Time this Week:	Hrs	Min	Goal for the Week: 3 Hrs

For audio, go to www.myovient.com and enter the audio code shown at the top of this page.

Syllable Stress Audio #80340

Do you remember the du-du-DA rhythm that you learned in Lesson 4? We can think of syllables in the same way. The du is an unstressed syllable, and the DA is a stressed syllable.

Match the following words to the correct stress pattern below: *application, analyst, authority, commission, community, confusion, dangerous, demonstration, disclosure, excellent, facility, graduation, hospital, material, motivation, philosophy, photographic, potential, practical, tradition*

1. **DA**-du-du (**STRESSED**-unstressed-unstressed)

2. du-**DA**-du (unstressed-**STRESSED**-unstressed)

3. du-'**DA**-du-**DA** (unstressed-**PRIMARY STRESS**-unstressed-**SECONDARY STRESS**)

4. **DA**-du-'**DA**-du (**SECONDARY STRESS**-unstressed-**PRIMARY STRESS**-unstressed)

Answers

1. **DA**-du-du: analyst, dangerous, excellent, hospital, practical; 2. du-**DA**-du: confusion, commission, disclosure, potential, tradition; 3. du-'**DA**-du-**DA**: authority, community, facility, material, philosophy; 4. **DA**-du-'**DA**-du: application, demonstration, graduation, motivation, photographic

☐ **Think of ten words that you use daily and write them here. Label their stress patterns.**

| Practice Time Today: | Hrs | Min | **Practice Time this Week:** | Hrs | Min | **Goal for the Week: 3 Hrs** |

Syllable Stress Audio #80350

Complete ☐

The following list shows the difference in syllable stress between certain nouns and verbs that have the same spelling. Read each word three times, stressing the correct syllable, and then try making a full sentence using that word.

SOUNDS
CONNECTIONS
RHYTHM

Nouns

☐ ☐ ☐ **ad**dress
☐ ☐ ☐ **all**y
☐ ☐ ☐ **con**duct
☐ ☐ ☐ **con**flict
☐ ☐ ☐ **con**test
☐ ☐ ☐ **con**vert
☐ ☐ ☐ **im**pact
☐ ☐ ☐ **in**sult
☐ ☐ ☐ **in**sert
☐ ☐ ☐ **ob**ject
☐ ☐ ☐ **per**mit
☐ ☐ ☐ **pres**ent
☐ ☐ ☐ **prog**ress
☐ ☐ ☐ **re**cap
☐ ☐ ☐ **re**cord
☐ ☐ ☐ **sub**ject
☐ ☐ ☐ **sur**vey
☐ ☐ ☐ **sus**pect
☐ ☐ ☐ **up**set

Verbs

☐ ☐ ☐ ad**dress**
☐ ☐ ☐ **all**y
☐ ☐ ☐ con**duct**
☐ ☐ ☐ con**flict**
☐ ☐ ☐ con**test**
☐ ☐ ☐ con**vert**
☐ ☐ ☐ im**pact**
☐ ☐ ☐ in**sult**
☐ ☐ ☐ in**sert**
☐ ☐ ☐ ob**ject**
☐ ☐ ☐ per**mit**
☐ ☐ ☐ pre**sent**
☐ ☐ ☐ pro**gress**
☐ ☐ ☐ re**cap**
☐ ☐ ☐ re**cord**
☐ ☐ ☐ sub**ject**
☐ ☐ ☐ sur**vey**
☐ ☐ ☐ sus**pect**
☐ ☐ ☐ up**set**

American English speakers often stress the first syllable of the following words. However, stressing the second syllable of some of these words is also acceptable, as shown below.

Nouns

☐ ☐ ☐ **ac**cent
☐ ☐ ☐ **con**tract
☐ ☐ ☐ **con**trast
☐ ☐ ☐ **de**tail/de**tail**
☐ ☐ ☐ **ex**port
☐ ☐ ☐ **pro**test
☐ ☐ ☐ **re**fund
☐ ☐ ☐ **re**search/re**search**

Verbs

☐ ☐ ☐ **ac**cent
☐ ☐ ☐ **con**tract/con**tract**
☐ ☐ ☐ **con**trast/con**trast**
☐ ☐ ☐ **de**tail/de**tail**
☐ ☐ ☐ **ex**port/ex**port**
☐ ☐ ☐ **pro**test/pro**test**
☐ ☐ ☐ **re**fund/re**fund**
☐ ☐ ☐ **re**search/re**search**

     For audio, go to www.myovient.com and enter the audio code shown at the top of this page.

Syllable Stress Audio #80360

☐ **Look at the following paragraph and underline the words that should be stressed in each sentence. Next, circle the stressed syllables in each of the words you have underlined. The first sentence has been done for you.**

SOUNDS

CONNECTIONS

RHYTHM

Do you ever look around you and wonder whether you are dressed appropriately for your job? Do you notice men coming to work without a tie and think they're underdressed? Dress codes in many companies today are relaxed, and in many cases "business-casual" clothing is normal. Khaki pants and shirts without ties are common and acceptable. This is especially true in professions where employees are not in face-to-face contact with customers. Some employees in more relaxed areas of business can even go to work in jeans and t-shirts. Even if their workplace requires more formal clothing, like suits and ties, they might have one day a week when employees can relax and dress down, usually called "casual Friday." The best way to understand how to dress for your workplace is to analyze what your coworkers are wearing. Whatever your company requires, be sure to wear clothing that feels good. That way, even if you don't like the dress code, at least you'll be comfortable!

☐ **Intonation tip: Add intonation to every word that is stressed and make sure the intonation goes UP on the stressed syllable.**

☐ **Record yourself reading this paragraph and listen to the recording. Has your pronunciation improved?**

Syllable Stress (Unstressed Syllables) Audio #80370

Complete

It is important to not only stress the correct syllable in your words but also to shorten the unstressed syllables. The vowels in the unstressed syllables usually get shortened to either an /ɪ/ sound or an /ə/ sound. Practice these examples. Pay careful attention to the sound of the unstressed syllables.

SOUNDS
CONNECTIONS
RHYTHM

☐ ☐ ☐ focus (FO-kɪs)   (not FO-cus)

☐ ☐ ☐ Oakland (OAK-lənd)   (not OAK-land)

☐ ☐ ☐ developer (də-VEL-əp-ər)   (not de-VEL-op-er)

☐ ☐ ☐ surface (SUR-fɪce)   (not SUR-face)

☐ ☐ ☐ design (də-SIGN)   (not de-SIGN)

☐ ☐ ☐ anniversary (an-nə-VER-sə-ry) (not an-ni-VER-sa-ry)

☐ ☐ ☐ climate (CLI-mət)   (not CLI-mate)

Some unstressed vowels are so weak that they disappear altogether.

☐ ☐ ☐ family (FAM-ly)   (not FAM-i-ly)

☐ ☐ ☐ comfortable (COMF-ter-bəl)   (not COM-fort-a-bul)

☐ ☐ ☐ camera (CAM-rə)   (not CAM-er-a)

☐ ☐ ☐ interesting (IN-trɪ-stɪng)   (not IN-ter-est-ing)

Practice Time Today: Hrs   Min   **Practice Time this Week:**   Hrs   Min   **Goal for the Week: 3 Hrs**

For audio, go to www.myovient.com and enter the audio code shown at the top of this page.

Syllable Stress Review

Complete ☐

☐ When you are practicing syllable stress, it is important to use other tools to help remind yourself to stress your syllables. Practice giving a short self-introduction speech and pull a rubber band apart when you say the stressed syllables. Record yourself.

☐ Listen to a native speaker on TV, the radio or the Internet. Focus on listening to the stressed syllables of the key words in his/her speech. Can you hear the stress?

☐ Write down words that you have trouble pronouncing. Where should the syllable stress go? Check the dictionary if you do not know. Are there any sounds that should be shortened? Look up the words in a dictionary. In the dictionary's pronunciation guide for the word, look for vowels that are written like /ɪ/ or /ə/. These are usually the unstressed syllables. Record yourself pronouncing these words. Pay careful attention to the unstressed sounds. Shorten these sounds.

Self-Reflection:

Write your feelings about your ability to stress the correct syllable in your words. Do you feel that you have been able to use these principles in your daily speech? Have you received any feedback about your pronunciation from friends or coworkers since you started this program?

Practice Time Today:	Hrs	Min	Practice Time this Week:	Hrs	Min	Goal for the Week: 3 Hrs

Rules for Connecting Sounds

Are There Specific Rules for Connecting Sounds Together?

Yes. In Lesson 3, you learned some basic concepts related to connecting, but there are several rules you can use to connect more accurately.

Consonants Connect to Vowels:	have a → hava
	meeting at → meetin-gat
	Aptos office → Apto-soffice
Vowels Connect to Vowels:	you and → you-wand
	the Aptos → th-yaptos
Consonants Connect to Consonants:	and Dave → anDave
	pass your → pass-shor

Are There Any Sounds That Change When They Connect?

Yes. When the first word ends in a /s/, /z/, /t/, or /d/ sound and the next word starts with a /j/ sound, the words are connected by a new sound. This only happens when the word with the /j/ sound is unstressed.

IPA	**Example**
/s/ + /j/ → /ʃ/	*Pass your paper* sounds like *pa-shor-paper*.
/z/ + /j/ → /ʒ/	*Ease your mind* sounds like *ea-zhor mind*.
/t/ + /j/ → /tʃ/	*Get your car* sounds like *ge-chor car*.
/d/ + /j/ → /dʒ/	*I can't find you* sounds like *I can't fin-jou*.

The letters inside the slashes (//) are IPA symbols. These represent a specific sound in English. Refer to the IPA chart in Appendix B to learn more about the IPA.

Do I Need to Memorize Special Connecting Rules?

No. The best way to learn and practice connecting is to simply extend the ends of your words and let them connect with the next word naturally. The rules are useful for helping you understand how words connect, but if you think too much about the rules while you are speaking, your speech will not sound fluent.

Instead of memorizing rules, try memorizing the sound connections in groups of words that you commonly use. This will make it easier to add connections to your speech more naturally.

If you want to add extra stress to an important word, do not connect the word to anything. Remember, pauses help highlight a word, so surrounding your important words with pauses (and no connections) will make them extra clear.

REVIEW
Answer these questions without looking at the notes on the left.

How do I connect consonants to vowels?

How do I connect vowels to vowels?

How do I connect consonants to consonants?

Do I need to memorize special connecting rules?

Goal for the Week: 3 Hrs

Connecting Rules
(Consonants to Vowels) Audio #80380

Complete ☐

Rule: When a word ends in a consonant and the next word begins with a vowel sound, connect the words with the consonant sound.

Practice connecting the words that end in consonants with the words that begin with vowels. Read each one three times.

| SOUNDS |
| CONNECTIONS |
| RHYTHM |

☐ ☐ ☐ email account   ☐ ☐ ☐ technological advantage

☐ ☐ ☐ president of the company   ☐ ☐ ☐ competitive environment

☐ ☐ ☐ business acumen   ☐ ☐ ☐ demand is growing

☐ ☐ ☐ unique approach   ☐ ☐ ☐ industry-wide initiatives

☐ ☐ ☐ reports and presentations   ☐ ☐ ☐ try to stand out

☐ ☐ ☐ recovers and utilizes   ☐ ☐ ☐ think of new ideas

☐ ☐ ☐ mind over matter   ☐ ☐ ☐ research and development

☐ ☐ ☐ cost increase   ☐ ☐ ☐ tools and supplies

☐ ☐ ☐ trust is earned   ☐ ☐ ☐ it's a result of the merger

For the items below, first mark the thought groups. Next, practice reading the sentences while connecting the consonants and vowels inside the thought groups. Read each one three times.

☐ ☐ ☐ Shares of the company rose 15 percent.

☐ ☐ ☐ The Dow Jones Industrial average is at an all-time high.

☐ ☐ ☐ Airplanes are lightening up in order to reduce fuel costs.

☐ ☐ ☐ Home equity loans are drying up for some people.

☐ ☐ ☐ Turning out the lights will help save energy costs.

☐ **Memorize one of the sentences above and practice saying it while looking in the mirror. Focus on connecting the sounds within the thought groups.**

Sometimes connecting can make your words sound like other words. However, your listeners will be able to understand your meaning by thinking about the context of your message.

Look old → Look cold   *Bad ear → Bad deer*   *Soup or → Super*
The sky → This guy   *Enough is → Enough fizz*   *Jump up → Jump pup*

| **Practice Time Today:** | Hrs | Min | **Practice Time this Week:** | Hrs | Min | **Goal for the Week: 3 Hrs** |

Connecting Rules
(Vowels to Vowels) Audio #80390

Complete ☐

Rule: When a word ends in an /i/ sound and the next word begins with a vowel, the words are connected by a light /j/ (pronounced "y") sound.

Practice connecting the words that end in vowels with the words that begin with vowels. Read each one three times.

☐ ☐ ☐ early adopter

☐ ☐ ☐ an alloy of bronze and zinc

☐ ☐ ☐ try out

☐ ☐ ☐ deploy a strategy

☐ ☐ ☐ today in business

☐ ☐ ☐ proprietary information

☐ ☐ ☐ lay over

☐ ☐ ☐ risky alternative

☐ ☐ ☐ finally agree

☐ ☐ ☐ pay out

Rule: When a word ends in a /u/ sound and the next word begins with a vowel, the words are connected by a light /w/ sound.

Practice connecting the words that end in vowels with the words that begin with vowels. Read each one three times.

☐ ☐ ☐ new architecture

☐ ☐ ☐ vow of silence

☐ ☐ ☐ tow away zone

☐ ☐ ☐ knew of him

☐ ☐ ☐ two options

☐ ☐ ☐ end to end

☐ ☐ ☐ now and then

☐ ☐ ☐ true answer

☐ ☐ ☐ who were

☐ ☐ ☐ allow unlimited access

For the items below, first mark the thought groups. Next, practice reading the sentences while connecting the vowels inside the thought groups. Read each one three times.

☐ ☐ ☐ The company had to change the way it did business.

☐ ☐ ☐ The company opted to deploy a new infrastructure.

☐ ☐ ☐ Because customers don't have to pay an annual fee, membership is way up.

☐ ☐ ☐ Although he knew it was illegal, he occasionally parked in a tow away zone.

☐ ☐ ☐ They had a powwow to see if they could finally agree on a new advisor.

☐ **Memorize one of the sentences above and practice saying it while looking in the mirror. Focus on connecting the sounds within the thought groups.**

Practice Time Today:	Hrs	Min	Practice Time this Week:	Hrs	Min	Goal for the Week: 3 Hrs

For audio, go to www.myovient.com and enter the audio code shown at the top of this page.

Lesson 7 / Practice Day 3

Connecting Rules
(Consonants to Consonants) Audio #80400

Complete ☐

Rule: When the first word ends in a consonant and the next word ends in the same consonant, pronounce the consonant only one time.

Practice connecting the words that end and begin with the same consonant sound. Read each one three times.

SOUNDS
CONNECTIONS
RHYTHM

☐ ☐ ☐ web browser

☐ ☐ ☐ hard drive

☐ ☐ ☐ custom made

☐ ☐ ☐ big game

☐ ☐ ☐ final limit

☐ ☐ ☐ service sector

☐ ☐ ☐ enterprise solutions

☐ ☐ ☐ year round

☐ ☐ ☐ put together

☐ ☐ ☐ business solutions

Rule: When a word ends in a consonant "stop" such as /p/, /b/, /t/, /d/, /k/, or /g/ sound, and the next words starts with a consonant "stop" or the /tʃ/ or /dʒ/ sound, do not release the air from the sound at the end of the first word. Instead, hold the air and release it at the beginning of the second word.

Practice connecting the words that end in consonant stops and begin with consonant stops. Read each one three times.

☐ ☐ ☐ best chance

☐ ☐ ☐ draft board

☐ ☐ ☐ don't judge

☐ ☐ ☐ weak choices

☐ ☐ ☐ give up bandwidth

☐ ☐ ☐ background (Linking occurs inside words, too!)

☐ ☐ ☐ demand growth

☐ ☐ ☐ analyst group

☐ ☐ ☐ can't justify

☐ ☐ ☐ observant personnel

For the items below, first mark the thought groups. Next, practice reading these sentences while connecting the consonants inside the thought groups. Read each one three times.

☐ ☐ ☐ Investors were discouraged by the data on new home sales.

☐ ☐ ☐ Your old notebook can still be put to use.

☐ ☐ ☐ Our first choice didn't accept the position, so we'll give it to our second choice.

☐ ☐ ☐ We need help discovering our competitive advantage.

☐ ☐ ☐ The help desk is always there when you need it to be.

☐ **Memorize one of the sentences above and practice saying it while looking in the mirror. Focus on connecting the sounds within the thought groups.**

Practice Time Today:	Hrs	Min	Practice Time this Week:	Hrs	Min	Goal for the Week: 3 Hrs

Connecting Rules
(Tongue Position Change) Audio #80410

Complete ☐

Rule: When a word ends in a /s/, /z/, /t/, or /d/ sound, and the next word starts with a /j/ sound, the words are connected by a new sound. This only happens when the "y" word is unstressed.

IPA	Example
/s/ + /j/ → /ʃ/	*Pass your paper* sounds like *pa-shor-paper*.
/z/ + /j/ → /ʒ/	*Ease your mind* sounds like *ea-zhor mind*.
/t/ + /j/ → /tʃ/	*Get your car* sounds like *ge-chor car*.
/d/ + /j/ → /dʒ/	*I can't find you* sounds like *I can't fin-jou*.

Practice connecting the words below by changing the sound. Read each one three times.

☐ ☐ ☐ understand your clients   ☐ ☐ ☐ trust your instincts

☐ ☐ ☐ could you   ☐ ☐ ☐ would you

☐ ☐ ☐ is your   ☐ ☐ ☐ miss your deadline

☐ ☐ ☐ not yet   ☐ ☐ ☐ last year

☐ ☐ ☐ find your strengths   ☐ ☐ ☐ read your mail

For the items below, first mark the thought groups. Next, practice reading the sentences while connecting the /s/, /z/, /t/, and /d/ sounds to the word that begins with "y." Read each one three times.

☐ ☐ ☐ Did you really understand your data?

☐ ☐ ☐ They raised 3 million dollars in Series A funding last year.

☐ ☐ ☐ Could you help me fix the bugs in the system?

☐ ☐ ☐ The first users of the product had to deal with many issues.

☐ ☐ ☐ The consultant should point you toward a realistic solution.

☐ **Memorize one of the sentences above and practice saying it while looking in the mirror. Focus on connecting the sounds within the thought groups.**

Practice Time Today: ___ Hrs ___ Min   **Practice Time this Week:** ___ Hrs ___ Min   **Goal for the Week: 3 Hrs**

   For audio, go to www.myovient.com and enter the audio code shown at the top of this page.

Connecting Rules Review Audio #80420   Complete ☐

Mark the places in this paragraph where you should pause. Analyze the thought groups and draw a line connecting the sounds that you think should be connected.

SOUNDS
CONNECTIONS
RHYTHM

Venture capitalists are important for start-up companies that are not

large enough to raise capital in the public markets or stable enough to qualify for

direct bank loans. The investors in these companies usually have a great deal of

say in how the companies will be run. Sand Hill Road in Menlo Park, California

is seen as a symbol of private capital, just as Wall Street is a symbol of the stock

market because of the large number of venture capital companies located there.

☐ ☐ **Read the paragraph two times and practice connecting the words between the pauses. If possible, record yourself and listen to the recording. Compare this recording with your recording from Lesson 1. Do you hear a difference?**

☐ **Listen to a native speaker on the radio, Internet or TV. Write down a few sentences that you hear. Underline places where you think there should be connections. Now listen again and check to see if the speaker actually connected those words.**

_____

_____

_____

_____

_____

_____

_____

| **Practice Time Today:** | Hrs | Min | **Practice Time this Week:** | Hrs | Min | **Goal for the Week: 3 Hrs** |

Connecting Rules Review Audio #80430

Complete

Write out a conversation that you might have with a coworker at work.

1) Mark the places where you might pause.

2) Analyze the dialog and underline the words that should be connected.

SOUNDS
CONNECTIONS
RHYTHM

Example:

A: Do you ha<u>ve a</u> minute | to talk?

B: Sure. | What<u>'s o</u>n your mind?

A: I wa<u>s w</u>ondering if | you ha<u>d a</u> chance to talk <u>to E</u>ve | abou<u>t the</u> projec<u>t d</u>eadline?

B: I just foun<u>d out</u> | tha<u>t it's o</u>kay | to move the deadline | to nex<u>t w</u>eek.

A: That's great. | Shoul<u>d I</u> tell the team?

B: No, | that<u>'s o</u>kay. | I'm going to sen<u>d everyone an email</u> | right now.

☐ ☐ **Read the example two times. Now write your own dialog.**

A: _____

B: _____

A: _____

B: _____

A: _____

B: _____

☐ ☐ ☐ **Read your dialog three times and record yourself. Did you remember to connect your words?**

| **Practice Time Today:** | Hrs | Min | **Practice Time this Week:** | Hrs | Min | **Goal for the Week: 3 Hrs** |

 For audio, go to www.myovient.com and enter the audio code shown at the top of this page.

Connecting Rules Review Audio #80440

Complete ☐

☐ **Look at the words below. Next to the words, write the sounds that should connect. Practice reading and connecting the sounds in the phrases.**

SOUNDS
CONNECTIONS
RHYTHM

new web browsers	a host of innovations
sit on	top of
inside of	security is
to worry about	you will
be able	forget your
your old	problems easily
what is	your opinion
the old	old browsers

☐ **Read the sentences below and practice reading them while connecting the sounds.**

1. New web browsers offer a host of innovations.

2. Some browsers sit on top of, rather than inside of, a computer's operating system.

3. Security is not the only thing to worry about.

4. You will be able to forget your old problems easily.

5. What is your opinion of the old browsers?

☐ **Review the self-introduction that you wrote in Lesson 1, Practice Day 3. Write it here. Mark the places where you should pause and underline the sounds that should connect. Record yourself giving your self-introduction, and check your connecting and pausing.**

For audio, go to www.myovient.com and enter the audio code shown at the top of this page.

Deleting and Reducing Sounds

What Does It Mean to "Delete" or "Reduce" a Sound?

When you eliminate a sound from inside a word, you are deleting the sound. For example, many native speakers delete the first "e" in the word *interesting*. They pronounce it with three syllables instead of four: *in-trest-ing*. When you change a full vowel sound into a smaller and shorter sound, you are "reducing" the sound. The "a" in the word *and* is usually reduced to the "i" sound in *it* when spoken quickly in a sentence.

When Do Native Speakers Delete and Reduce Sounds?

Native speakers often reduce the unstressed vowel sounds in words. In addition, the sounds at the ends of words are often linked to the words that follow. However, when native speakers want to speak clearly (in a presentation, for example), they will choose not to delete and reduce sounds so that their audience does not misunderstand them. Deletions and reductions typically happen in casual or in fast speech. (For example, people will say "I dunno" instead of "I don't know.")

Do I Have to Follow These Rules?

No, you do not have to follow these rules when you speak. You should focus on pronouncing all of your sounds clearly, but using these rules in casual conversations can help you sound more fluent. Knowing these rules, however, will help you become a better listener. Native speakers can be difficult to understand because they often delete sounds within words, change vowel sounds, and connect words together.

When Should I Use These Rules?

You can use these rules when speaking casually. We usually speak this way with family and friends. There are a few words that you can memorize and always pronounce with deletions or reductions. When speaking formally, trying to make a good first impression, or giving a formal speech or presentation, you should avoid deleting and reducing sounds.

Can I Use Deletion and Reduction in My Writing?

No. You should not remove sounds or words when you are writing. These pronunciation patterns are only used in spoken English. There is one exception to this rule, however. When you write text messages and messages on online social networking sites, you can use these deletion and reduction patterns. For example "Whatcha doin?" and "Where r u?" are common ways of writing "What are you doing?" and "Where are you?" in texts.

REVIEW
Answer these questions without looking at the notes on the left.

What is deleting and reducing?

When do native speakers do this?

Do I have to follow these rules?

When should I use these rules?

Can I use deletion and reduction in my writing?

Goal for the Week: 3 Hrs

     For audio, go to www.myovient.com and enter the audio code shown at the top of this page.

Deleting Sounds Audio #80450

Practice reading these sentences three times each. Underline the key words in each sentence. Notice that we only delete sounds in words that are NOT stressed.

Deleted Letter "H" (This happens with the words *he*, *him*, *his*, *her* & also with the "th" in *them*.)

☐ ☐ ☐ I saw him in his cube. → I saw 'im in 'is cube.
☐ ☐ ☐ I think he went to the headquarters. → I think 'e went to the headquarters.
☐ ☐ ☐ Do you think he cares? → Do you think 'e cares?

☐ ☐ ☐ Your example: _____

> When you delete a letter, be sure to blend the letters before and after it together. "In his" should sound like "innis."

Deleted Letter "D" (This happens with the word *and*.)

☐ ☐ ☐ I work for the R and D division. → I work for the R an' D division.
☐ ☐ ☐ We had wine and cheese at the party. → We had wine an' cheese at the party.
☐ ☐ ☐ Follow up with an email and phone call. → Follow up with an email an' phone call.

☐ ☐ ☐ Your example: _____

Deleted Letter "T" (This often happens when a word ends with the letter *t*. Put your tongue into the *t* position and stop the sound with your throat instead of pushing the air out of your mouth. This is also called a *glottal stop*. See page 89 for more practice. When a word begins with the prefix *inter-*, the /t/ becomes an /n/ sound.)

☐ ☐ ☐ I can't seem to get this page to open. → I can'(t) seem to ge(t) this page to open.
☐ ☐ ☐ Internet shopping is very convenient. → In(t)erne(t) shopping is very convenien(t).
☐ ☐ ☐ The report was known internationally. → The repor(t) was known in(t)ernationally.

☐ ☐ ☐ Your example: _____

Deleted Letter "G" (This often happens with words ending in *ing*.)

☐ ☐ ☐ I think everyone is getting a pay raise. → I think everyone is gettin' a pay raise.
☐ ☐ ☐ It's going very well. → It's goin' very well.

☐ ☐ ☐ Your example: _____

Deleted Vowels The middle vowel is sometimes silent in three- or four-syllable words. (See page 59.)

☐ ☐ ☐ family →"fam-ly"   ☐ ☐ ☐ general →"gen-rul"
☐ ☐ ☐ usually →"u-zhu-ly"   ☐ ☐ ☐ comfortable →"comf-ter-bul"
☐ ☐ ☐ conference →"con-frence"   ☐ ☐ ☐ interest →"in-trest"

Other Deletions Letters are sometimes deleted in order to make difficult sounds easier to pronounce.

☐ ☐ ☐ fifth →"fith"   ☐ ☐ ☐ sandwich →"san-wich"   ☐ ☐ ☐ clothes →"close"

Practice Time Today:	Hrs	Min	**Practice Time this Week:**	Hrs	Min	**Goal for the Week: 3 Hrs**

Deleting Sounds (Contractions) Audio #80460   Complete ☐

When we speak, we often use contractions like "can't" or "I've." We pronounce contractions just like they are spelled, not like the original words. Practice pronouncing these contractions.

is = 's	has = 's		had = 'd	have = 've	are = 're
he's	he's		I'd	I've	we're
she's	she's		we'd	we've	they're
it's	it's		you'd	you've	you're
there's	there's		he'd	they've	
that's	that's		she'd		
where's	where's		they'd		

not = n't

isn't	doesn't	can't	don't	aren't	didn't	wouldn't
won't	wasn't	couldn't	weren't	shouldn't	mustn't	mightn't

will = 'll	would = 'd	Also:
I'll	I'd	I am → I'm
we'll	we'd	Let us → Let's
you'll	you'd	
he'll	he'd	
she'll	she'd	
they'll	they'd	

The following contractions often sound like other words.

Original Word	Contraction	Sounds Like *(The italicized words are not real words.)*
I will	I'll	aisle / all
You will	you'll	Yule / *yul*
He will	he'll	heel / hill
We will	we'll	wheel / will
She will	she'll	*shiel* / shill
You are	you're	your / *yer*
They are	they're	there
We are	we're	*weir* / were
He would/he had	he'd	heed
We would/had	we'd	weed
We have	we've	weave
Why will	why'll	while
How will	how'll	howl
Who is/has	who's	whose
How is/has	how's	house (As a verb, it sounds like *howz*.)
Where is/has	where's	wears
Where are	where're	wearer
Why are	why're	wire
Why would/had	why'd	wide
Why is/has	why's	wise

☐ **Use contractions to make a few of your own sentences. Practice pronouncing the contractions in your sentences.**

Practice Time Today:	Hrs	Min	Practice Time this Week:	Hrs	Min	Goal for the Week: 3 Hrs

For audio, go to www.myovient.com and enter the audio code shown at the top of this page.

Reducing Sounds Audio #80470

Complete ☐

In the unstressed words in a sentence, the vowel sounds often change. In these words, the vowels become /ə/ or /ɪ/. (See Appendix B for a pronunciation guide for these symbols.)

Because they are weak sounds, we say that we are "reducing" the sound.

Original Word	Reduced Sound	Example
you	/jə/	What are <u>you</u> doing?
your	/jər/	<u>Your</u> copies are finished.
to	/tə/ (Sometimes /də/)	Talk <u>to</u> your manager.
or	/ər/	Want coffee <u>or</u> tea?
can	/kɪn/	I <u>can</u> go with you.

You cannot delete or reduce sounds if the word is the first word in the sentence or a stressed keyword.

Read these questions three times each. Practice reducing the sounds in the underlined words.

☐ ☐ ☐ When are <u>you</u> moving?

☐ ☐ ☐ Did <u>you</u> get my message?

☐ ☐ ☐ What's <u>your</u> son's name?

☐ ☐ ☐ Is <u>your</u> computer backed up?

☐ ☐ ☐ Who did <u>you</u> give it to? (*To* is not reduced here because it is a stressed word.)

☐ ☐ ☐ Do you have <u>to</u> miss the meeting?

☐ ☐ ☐ Did <u>you</u> park in the front <u>or</u> the back?

☐ ☐ ☐ What <u>can</u> you do about it?

☐ ☐ ☐ Your example: _____

☐ ☐ ☐ Your example: _____

☐ ☐ ☐ Your example: _____

☐ **Think of a time when you were shopping or eating at a restaurant and had bad customer service. Tell this story to a friend or tell it to yourself while looking in a mirror. Practice reducing your vowel sounds in the unstressed words. Next, record yourself speaking. Listen to your recording and check to make sure you reduced the vowels in the unstressed words.**

Practice Time Today:	Hrs	Min	Practice Time this Week:	Hrs	Min	Goal for the Week: 3 Hrs

Deleting and Reducing Sounds Audio #80480

Complete

☐ **Look at the following paragraph and read the underlined words as they are written. The underlined words represent words with commonly reduced vowel sounds.**

Enid was an engineer noted <u>fer 'er</u> research in computer network security systems. Although she often analyzed complicated attacks on computers, the security system <u>fer 'er</u> house baffled <u>'er</u>. When she first installed <u>'er</u> own alarm system, she avoided <u>turnin'</u> it on because it beeped at regular intervals <u>an'</u> bothered <u>'er</u>. She believed that a system wasn't needed <u>fer 'er</u> house. She felt that <u>'er</u> neighborhood was safe. But after <u>hearin'</u> that a thief had climbed through a neighbor's back window <u>an'</u> robbed <u>'im</u> of $500, she finally asked a technician <u>fer</u> help.

☐ **Write a paragraph about someone you know who has had something stolen. What happened? (If you do not have a story to tell, make one up!) After writing it, underline all the words that could have reduced or deleted sounds. Record yourself reading it. Can you hear the reductions and deletions?**

_____

_____

_____

_____

_____

_____

_____

| **Practice Time Today:** | Hrs | Min | **Practice Time this Week:** | Hrs | Min | **Goal for the Week: 3 Hrs** |

Deleting and Reducing Sounds Audio #80490

Complete ☐

Common Phrases: The sounds in the phrases below often change in casual speech. You should avoid this kind of speech when you are speaking in formal situations (like at work), but you can use these phrases when you are talking with friends, when you are texting, or when writing messages on social networking sites.

SOUNDS
CONNECTIONS
RHYTHM

☐ ☐ ☐ Going to → Gonna   ☐ ☐ ☐ We're gonna pick up the dry cleaning.

☐ ☐ ☐ I am going to → I'mana   ☐ ☐ ☐ I'mana talk to him.

☐ ☐ ☐ Want to → Wanna   ☐ ☐ ☐ I wanna go to lunch.

☐ ☐ ☐ Have to → Hafta   ☐ ☐ ☐ I hafta get a new computer.

☐ ☐ ☐ Got to → Gotta   ☐ ☐ ☐ I've gotta call him.

☐ ☐ ☐ Ought to → Oughtta   ☐ ☐ ☐ He oughtta talk to her.

☐ ☐ ☐ Kind of → Kinda   ☐ ☐ ☐ I kinda like it.

☐ ☐ ☐ Could have → Coulda   ☐ ☐ ☐ I coulda gotten the discount if I had asked.

☐ ☐ ☐ Would have → Woulda   ☐ ☐ ☐ She woulda wanted me to do it.

☐ ☐ ☐ Should have → Shoulda ☐ ☐ ☐ I shoulda stayed on my diet.

☐ ☐ ☐ Might have → Mighta   ☐ ☐ ☐ I mighta known.

☐ ☐ ☐ Don't know → Dunno   ☐ ☐ ☐ I dunno why she left her job.

☐ ☐ ☐ What are you → Whatcha ☐ ☐ ☐ Whatcha doing this weekend?

☐ ☐ ☐ Give me → Gimme   ☐ ☐ ☐ Gimme another chance.

☐ ☐ ☐ Let me → Lemme   ☐ ☐ ☐ Lemme try it again.

Write example sentences using some of these phrases. Practice reading each one three times.

☐ ☐ ☐ _____

☐ ☐ ☐ _____

☐ ☐ ☐ _____

☐ ☐ ☐ _____

☐ ☐ ☐ _____

☐ ☐ ☐ _____

Practice Time Today:	Hrs	Min	**Practice Time this Week:**	Hrs	Min	**Goal for the Week: 3 Hrs**

For audio, go to www.myovient.com and enter the audio code shown at the top of this page.

Deletion and Reduction Audio #80500

Complete

☐ **Find all the possible deleted and reduced sounds in these sentences. Write the changes on the right.**

What is your future?

_____

Will you spend your life

_____

working for someone else?

_____

Or, are you brave enough

_____

to start your own business?

_____

Starting your own business

_____

requires courage,

_____

perseverance,

_____

and optimism.

_____

Do you have what it takes?

_____

SOUNDS

CONNECTIONS

RHYTHM

☐ **Read the sentences again with the changes you have made. Record yourself and check your pronunciation progress.**

Answers:

What's yer future? Will ya spend yer life workin' fer someone else? Er, are ya brave enough ta start yer own business? Startin' yer own business requires courage, perseverance an' optimism. Do ya have what it takes?

☐ **Many people match their pronunciation to the local style of their audience. This is often done as a way to connect to the audience by showing the audience that the speaker is part of the same social or economic group. Politicians are famous for doing this. Do a search on the Internet for some famous politicians like George Bush or Bill Clinton. See if you can hear any deletions or vowel reductions in their speech. Write some of the phrases you hear below.**

_____

_____

_____

_____

_____

Practice Time Today: Hrs   Min   **Practice Time this Week:**   Hrs   Min   **Goal for the Week: 3 Hrs**

For audio, go to www.myovient.com and enter the audio code shown at the top of this page.

Lesson 8 / Practice Day 7

Linking, Deletion & Reduction Review Audio #80510

Complete ☐

SOUNDS
CONNECTIONS
RHYTHM

☐ **Read these questions and add linking, deletion, and reduction where possible.**

1. What is your name?
2. Where are you from?
3. What do you do?
4. Where do you work?
5. What did you do last weekend?

☐ **Write 5 questions that you often ask people at your workplace. Add linking, deletion, and reduction and practice saying the questions without reading them.**

1) _____

2) _____

3) _____

4) _____

5) _____

☐ **Listen to a recording of a native speaker from a podcast or video (about 1 minute). Listen to the recording again and listen for any linking, deletion, or reduction. Write some of the phrases you hear below.**

_____

_____

_____

_____

Self-Reflection:

Write your feelings about your linking, sound deletion, and sound reduction progress. Do you feel that you have been able to use these principles in your speech? Have you received any feedback about your pronunciation from friends or coworkers since you started this program?

_____

_____

_____

Practice Time Today:	Hrs	Min	Practice Time this Week:	Hrs	Min	Goal for the Week: 3 Hrs

Individual Sounds

How Are "Sounds" Different from "Letters"?

Every letter of the English alphabet has a name. For example, the letter "f" is pronounced /ɛf/ when we say the name of the letter. If you spelled the word fan, you would say /ɛf/-/eɪ/-/ɛn/ (f-a-n). On the other hand, when we talk about sounds, we are talking about how the letter is pronounced inside of a word. When we pronounce the sound of "f" we say /f/ rather than /ɛf/.

There are nearly twice as many sounds in English as letters. This is because some letters have multiple sounds. For example, the sound of the letter "a" is different in these words: cap, fate, and pasta. The sound of the letters "th" are different in these words: bath and bathe.

What Is the International Phonetic Alphabet?

The International Phonetic Alphabet (IPA) is a standard set of symbols that represent sounds. For example, the sound that the letters "sh" make is written as /ʃ/ in the IPA. Although the same letter can be pronounced with different sounds in English, IPA symbols never change sounds. This means that you can use IPA to easily learn how to pronounce a new word. You can find these symbols in most dictionaries.

Can I Learn the Sound of a Word by Looking at Its Spelling?

Not always. Words are often not pronounced like they are spelled. For example, the "o" in college is pronounced with an "ah" sound, not an "o" sound. When you are practicing pronunciation, try not to focus too much on the word's individual letters. Instead, think of the whole word. Use the IPA symbols in your dictionary to check your pronunciation or ask a native speaker to help you.

How Important Are These Sounds?

The way you pronounce individual sounds is not the most important pronunciation skill. If you mispronounce a sound, your listener may still be able to guess what word you are saying based on the context or situation. However, it is a good idea to improve your sounds so that your listener does not have to work as hard to understand you. This is especially important in words that are similar except for one sound (star/store, light/right, fan/pan, for example).

Why Does It Feel Strange to Pronounce These Sounds?

In order to change your pronunciation, you need to move your mouth in new ways. If you are pronouncing sounds correctly for the first time, your mouth SHOULD feel strange.

How Can I Change the Way I Pronounce English Sounds?

To change your pronunciation, you first need to <u>hear</u> the difference. Next, you need to <u>practice</u> the sound many times. Then you need to <u>remind</u> yourself to say the sound correctly when you are speaking. After a lot of practice, you will be able to produce the sound without thinking about it.

You are attempting to change a habit, and it cannot happen overnight. It could take months of daily practice to change the way you make a sound. Be patient!

REVIEW
Answer these questions without looking at the notes on the left.

What is the difference between a sound and a letter?

What is the IPA?

Can I learn the sound of a word by looking at its spelling?

Why should I improve individual sounds?

Is it okay if my mouth feels strange?

How can I change my pronunciation?

Goal for the Week: 3 Hrs

Individual Sounds Audio #80520

Complete ☐

☐ **Look at the list of IPA (International Phonetic Alphabet) symbols and practice pronouncing each one. Notice where your tongue is in your mouth and how your mouth is shaped. Record yourself and compare your pronunciation with a native speaker's pronunciation.**

SOUNDS
CONNECTIONS
RHYTHM

Consonants		Vowels	
s	security	i	meeting
z	zoom	ɪ	Internet
ʃ	flash	ɛ	edge
ʒ	measure	æ	app
t	turn	ɑ	processor
ʔ	button	ɔ	caught
d	modern	u	virtual
tʃ	chip	ʊ	would
dʒ	just	ə	account
p	profit	ʌ	cut
b	benefit	eɪ	make
f	format	aɪ	client
v	virtual	aʊ	however
θ	think	ɔɪ	noise
ð	this	oʊ	know
k	cable		
g	grant		
m	motor		
n	new		
ŋ	ring		
l	light		
r	right		
w	would		
j	yell		
h	how		

☐ **Make a list of words that you have trouble pronouncing. Look in a dictionary and write the IPA symbols for each word. Practice pronouncing the words.**

Ex) patent → p æ t ɛ n t

_____ → _____

_____ → _____

_____ → _____

_____ → _____

_____ → _____

_____ → _____

_____ → _____

_____ → _____

_____ → _____

☐ **Keep a notebook with you at all times to write down words that you mispronounce or that you cannot pronounce. You will know that you have mispronounced a word when someone asks you to repeat yourself.**

Review this list often. Are you having problems with the same sounds? Do you see improvement?

| **Practice Time Today:** | Hrs | Min | **Practice Time this Week:** | Hrs | Min | **Goal for the Week: 3 Hrs** |

Individual Sounds
(Voiced and Unvoiced Sounds) Audio #80530

Complete

Imagine that you are whispering to someone because you need to be very quiet. When you do this, you are not using your vocal cords or voice. You are just blowing air out of your mouth. Some English sounds are pronounced this way.

SOUNDS
CONNECTIONS
RHYTHM

☐ **Touch your hand to your throat and whisper this sentence: "I am not using my voice."** You should not feel any vibration in your throat. Now, put your fingers over your ears so that you cannot hear. **Whisper it again: "I am not using my voice."** You should not be able to hear yourself. This is because you are not using your vocal cords.

☐ **Touch your hand to your throat and say this sentence at your normal volume: "I am using my voice."** You should feel vibrations in your throat. Now, put your fingers over your ears so that you cannot hear. **Say it again: "I am using my voice."** You should hear your voice because you are using your vocal cords.

Sounds that do not use your vocal cords are called **unvoiced sounds**. Sounds that use your vocal cords are called **voiced sounds**.

These sounds are unvoiced: /s/, /ʃ/, /t/, /ʔ/, /tʃ/, /p/, /f/, /θ/, /k/, /h/

These sounds are voiced: /z/, /ʒ/, /d/, /dʒ/, /b/, /v/, /ð/, /g/, /m/, /n/, /ŋ/, /l/, /r/, /j/, /w/ + all vowels

Did you notice that some of the voiced and unvoiced sounds are made using similar tongue and jaw positions? The following sounds are "partner" sounds. Both sounds in each pair are formed the same way in your mouth, but one sound is voiced and the other is unvoiced.

Practice transforming the unvoiced sounds to voiced sounds by adding vibration from your vocal cords. Practice each pair five times.

	Unvoiced	Voiced
☐☐☐☐☐	s	z
☐☐☐☐☐	ʃ	ʒ
☐☐☐☐☐	t	d
☐☐☐☐☐	tʃ	dʒ
☐☐☐☐☐	p	b
☐☐☐☐☐	f	v
☐☐☐☐☐	θ	ð
☐☐☐☐☐	k	g

☐ **Practice these tongue twisters and pay attention to the voiced and unvoiced sounds.**

f (unvoiced) / v (voiced)
Five valuable vases were valued at fifteen billion.

s (unvoiced) / z (unvoiced)
The six sisters zipped to the city zoo.

p (unvoiced) / b (voiced)
Pam bans people from blasting punk beats.

| Practice Time Today: | Hrs | Min | **Practice Time this Week:** | Hrs | Min | **Goal for the Week: 3 Hrs** |

For audio, go to www.myovient.com and enter the audio code shown at the top of this page.

Individual Sounds (V, F, W, B, and P) Audio #80540   Complete ☐

Do you pronounce the first letter of these words differently: _vile_ – _file_ – _while_ – _bile_ – _pile_? **You should. These sounds are different.**

☐ **Practice these sounds. Look in the mirror and check your teeth and lip position.**

SOUNDS
CONNECTIONS
RHYTHM

/v/ sound: (Voiced) Your top teeth touch your bottom lip. Blow air out with a sound.

/f/ sound: (Unvoiced) Your top teeth touch your bottom lip. Blow air out without a sound.

/w/ sound: (Voiced) Make a small circle with your lips and then expand it. Do not use your teeth.

/b/ sound: (Voiced) Press your lips together and then separate as you make a voiced sound.

/p/ sound: (Unvoiced) Press your lips together and then separate as you blow air out without a sound.

Practice these words five times each. Look in the mirror and check your teeth and lip position.

/v/ : ☐☐☐☐☐ leave   ☐☐☐☐☐ live   ☐☐☐☐☐ level
          ☐☐☐☐☐ oven   ☐☐☐☐☐ value

/f/ : ☐☐☐☐☐ leaf   ☐☐☐☐☐ life   ☐☐☐☐☐ awful
          ☐☐☐☐☐ laugh   ☐☐☐☐☐ felt

/w/ : ☐☐☐☐☐ will   ☐☐☐☐☐ wife   ☐☐☐☐☐ welcome
          ☐☐☐☐☐ wow   ☐☐☐☐☐ wise

/b/ : ☐☐☐☐☐ lab   ☐☐☐☐☐ bite   ☐☐☐☐☐ able
          ☐☐☐☐☐ belt   ☐☐☐☐☐ best

/p/ : ☐☐☐☐☐ lap   ☐☐☐☐☐ pile   ☐☐☐☐☐ apple
          ☐☐☐☐☐ pelt   ☐☐☐☐☐ pest

Read these sentences three times each. Pay attention to the V, F, W, B, and P sounds.

☐☐☐ Please leave the oven off if you don't plan to use it.

☐☐☐ The cab driver smiled when I tipped him well.

☐☐☐ Phone applications are more popular than ever.

☐☐☐ Live life to the fullest every day.

☐☐☐ Welcome to our first ever benefit party.

☐☐☐ Put your best foot forward to leave a positive impression.

☐ **Choose one sound that is difficult for you and write it on a note card. Place this note card somewhere you will see it every day (on your desk, refrigerator, bathroom mirror). Every time you see the card, remind yourself to pronounce the sound clearly and correctly.**

Practice Time Today:	Hrs	Min	Practice Time this Week:	Hrs	Min	Goal for the Week: 3 Hrs

Individual Sounds (L, R, N, and M) Audio #80550   Complete ☐

Do you pronounce these words differently: *light – right?* **You should. These sounds are different.**

☐ **Practice these sounds. Look in the mirror and check your teeth, tongue and lip position.**

SOUNDS
CONNECTIONS
RHYTHM

/l/ sound at the beginning of a word: Put the tip of your tongue just behind the front top teeth. Make a voiced sound as you drop it down and begin the next vowel sound. (If you have trouble with this sound, stick your tongue outside your mouth to practice.)

/l/ sound in the middle or at the end of a word: First, make a small "uh" sound while pulling your tongue back a bit. Then, as you continue the "uh" sound, put the tip of your tongue just behind the front top teeth hold your tongue in this position as you finish the sound.

/r/ sound at the beginning of a word: Make an "o" shape with your lips. Pull your tongue up and back. Make a voiced sound while tensing your tongue. Do not let the tip of your tongue touch the top of your mouth! Begin the next vowel sound from this position.

/r/ sound in the middle or at the end of a word: Move from the previous vowel sound into the "r" by pulling your tongue to the back of your mouth. Do not let the tip of your tongue touch the top of your mouth! Make a voiced sound while tensing your tongue.

/n/ sound: Press the tip or front half of your tongue against the top of your mouth just behind your teeth. Hold your tongue in this position and make a voiced sound through your nose.

/m/ sound: Press your lips together and make a voiced sound through your nose.

Practice these words five times each. Look in the mirror and check your teeth and lip position.

/l/ : ☐☐☐☐☐ lock   ☐☐☐☐☐ golf   ☐☐☐☐☐ call
          ☐☐☐☐☐ light   ☐☐☐☐☐ polite

/r/ : ☐☐☐☐☐ rock   ☐☐☐☐☐ credit   ☐☐☐☐☐ car
          ☐☐☐☐☐ right   ☐☐☐☐☐ portrait

/n/ : ☐☐☐☐☐ knock   ☐☐☐☐☐ and   ☐☐☐☐☐ noun
          ☐☐☐☐☐ night   ☐☐☐☐☐ candy

/m/ : ☐☐☐☐☐ mock   ☐☐☐☐☐ lemon   ☐☐☐☐☐ mom
          ☐☐☐☐☐ might   ☐☐☐☐☐ amount

Read these sentences three times each. Pay attention to the L and R.

☐☐☐ Lock the golf clubs in your car trunk.

☐☐☐ Laughter is the best way to relieve stress.

☐☐☐ Technology is not a silver bullet.

☐☐☐ Don't mock me for trying to improve.

☐☐☐ Nothing is worse than being woken up by a phone call at one in the morning.

☐ **Choose a difficult sound to practice. Set an alert on your cell phone so that it rings every hour. When you hear the alert, practice the sound. Continue this until you have mastered the sound.**

Practice Time Today:	Hrs	Min	Practice Time this Week:	Hrs	Min	Goal for the Week: 3 Hrs

For audio, go to www.myovient.com and enter the audio code shown at the top of this page.

Individual Sounds (TH) Audio #80560   **Complete** ☐

Do you pronounce the "TH" differently in these word pairs: *thank* – *this* **and** *bath* – *bathe*? **You should. These sounds are different.**

SOUNDS
CONNECTIONS
RHYTHM

☐ **Practice these sounds. Look in the mirror and check your teeth, tongue and lip position.**

/θ/ sound: (Unvoiced) Put your tongue between your top and bottom teeth, blow air out without your voice. (If you have trouble with this sound, stick your tongue outside your mouth to practice.)

/ð/ sound: (Voiced) Put your tongue between your top and bottom teeth, blow air out with your voice. This sound will vibrate your tongue. (If you have trouble with this sound, stick your tongue outside your mouth to practice.)

Imagine that you have to make the sound in front of your mouth. If you look in a mirror, you should see your tongue sticking out a little.

Practice these words five times each. Look in the mirror and check your tongue position.

/θ/ : ☐☐☐☐☐ think   ☐☐☐☐☐ thin   ☐☐☐☐☐ thought
        ☐☐☐☐☐ month   ☐☐☐☐☐ south

/ð/ : ☐☐☐☐☐ this   ☐☐☐☐☐ than   ☐☐☐☐☐ though
        ☐☐☐☐☐ other   ☐☐☐☐☐ that

Read these sentences three times each. Make sure your tongue is between your teeth when you pronounce the TH sound.

☐☐☐ I don't think that this thesis has been thought through thoroughly.

☐☐☐ Thank you for thinking of me on my birthday.

☐☐☐ That was very thoughtful of you.

☐☐☐ Bathing suits are difficult to buy in cold weather months.

☐☐☐ The Olympic athlete was not thrilled to have placed fifth.

☐☐☐ It's important to think about your pronunciation throughout the day.

Attach practice to a habit! Choose any sound that is difficult for you and practice it every time you do something like wash your hands, check your email, get out of your desk chair, or make a phone call.

Pronunciation Check: Are you remembering to pause between thought groups and stretch your sounds at the ends of thought groups? If you are forgetting to do this, reread the sentences above and add pausing and stretching. While you are practicing your sounds, remember to maintain your rhythm.

Practice Time Today:	Hrs	Min	Practice Time this Week:	Hrs	Min	Goal for the Week: 3 Hrs

Individual Sounds (Double Vowels) Audio #80570   Complete ☐

Do you pronounce the vowels in these words differently: *wow – why* and *boy – no?* **You should. These sounds are different.**

☐ **Practice pronouncing these sounds. Look in the mirror and make sure your mouth first opens up wide then closes when you pronounce these sounds.**

SOUNDS
CONNECTIONS
RHYTHM

/aʊ/ sound: Start with your mouth open wide and make the /a/ sound. Then close your mouth and make the /u/ sound. Blend the two sounds together smoothly.

/aɪ/ sound: Start with your mouth open wide and make the /a/ sound. Then smile, pull your tongue back and make the /i/ sound. Blend the two sounds together smoothly.

/ɔɪ/ sound: Start with your lips in a wide circle say "oh." Then smile, pull your tongue back and make the /i/ sound. Blend the two sounds together smoothly.

/oʊ/ sound: Start with your lips in a wide circle say "oh." Then make the circle smaller and make the /u/ sound. Blend the two sounds together smoothly.

Tip: Close two fingers together and hold them horizontally next to your mouth. This is your mouth "measuring stick." Look in the mirror as you do this. When you practice these double vowel sounds, your mouth should open wider than your two fingers at the beginning and then close.

Practice these words five times each. Look in the mirror and make sure your mouth is moving from an open position to a closed position.

/aʊ/: ☐☐☐☐☐ now   ☐☐☐☐☐ cow   ☐☐☐☐☐ out
       ☐☐☐☐☐ found   ☐☐☐☐☐ south

/aɪ/ : ☐☐☐☐☐ tie   ☐☐☐☐☐ revise   ☐☐☐☐☐ why
       ☐☐☐☐☐ fly   ☐☐☐☐☐ guy

/ɔɪ/ : ☐☐☐☐☐ noise   ☐☐☐☐☐ toy   ☐☐☐☐☐ boy
       ☐☐☐☐☐ annoy   ☐☐☐☐☐ oil

/oʊ/ : ☐☐☐☐☐ alone   ☐☐☐☐☐ go   ☐☐☐☐☐ own
       ☐☐☐☐☐ snow   ☐☐☐☐☐ know

☐ **Underline all of the double vowel sounds in this paragraph. Read it aloud and record yourself. Open your mouth wide for all the vowel sounds.**

In order to organize your life, you must prioritize your goals. First, think about why you want to organize your life. Do you need more time for home? Did you vow to find joy in life before you die? Now, write your goals down in order from the highest priority to the lowest priority. Next, find a friend for support who will not be annoyed but will enjoy helping you reach your goals. Tell her why you want to try to prioritize your life. When you are tired of trying, your friend should remind you of your priorities. Finally, revise your priorities every now and then, but don't compromise or forgo your goals.

| **Practice Time Today:** | Hrs | Min | **Practice Time this Week:** | Hrs | Min | **Goal for the Week: 3 Hrs** |

Individual Sounds Audio #80580

Complete

What are ten words that you commonly use in conversations at work? Make a list of these words and write the IPA symbols for each word. (Check your dictionary.) Is there a sound in each word that is difficult for you to pronounce? Write it down. Record yourself pronouncing these words. Practice pronouncing each word 10 times.

If you do not know what sounds to focus on, ask a friend or teacher to diagnose your problems.

Word	IPA Symbols	Problem Sound	☐ Practice 10 Times
1.			☐
2.			☐
3.			☐
4.			☐
5.			☐
6.			☐
7.			☐
8.			☐
9.			☐
10.			☐

Review

☐ **Read this paragraph and practice all of the skills you have learned so far. Record yourself and listen to the recording. Rate your pausing, stretching, stress, connections, and sounds.**

Being 'green' isn't as hard as you think. There are many things that people can do quite easily to reduce the amount of damage they do to the environment. Whether it's turning down the thermostat or switching over to energy efficient light bulbs, almost everyone can make a difference by doing something small. Although you may have accomplished these first steps toward saving the planet, here are some more things you might want to consider. One, recycle your used printer cartridges—thousands of these end up in landfills throughout the country. Two, inform your community. Invite green experts to talk at your local community center. Try to make a real difference within your zip code. Three, get outside. Depending on the weather, go outdoors for your entertainment. Instead of visiting an air-conditioned movie theater, gather some friends and go for a hike or a picnic.

Practice Time Today:	Hrs	Min	**Practice Time this Week:**	Hrs	Min	**Goal for the Week: 3 Hrs**

Word Endings

SOUNDS
CONNECTIONS
RHYTHM

What Do Word Endings Tell Us?

The sounds at the ends of words give the listener information about the tense and number of the word. The meaning of the word can change depending on the ending:

They wait for the call. (Habit)   Give me the paper. (One paper)

They waited for the call. (Past)   Give me the papers. (Multiple papers)

Why Do Native English Speakers Have Problems Understanding Nonnative Speakers' Word Endings?

If people have trouble understanding your word endings, you are probably not holding the final sound long enough. Or, you may be adding an extra vowel sound when the word ends in a consonant. Here are a few common mistakes:

Word	Mistake	Tip to Make Your Pronunciation Better
Hall	Haa	Hold tongue longer at the top of your mouth.
Car	Caa	Tense tongue at the back of your mouth.
Green	Gree	Breathe through nose while pronouncing "n."
Back	Ba	Blow air out after the "k" sound.
Search	Searchi	Keep "ch" voiceless and do not add a vowel.
Stop	Stopu	Keep "p" voiceless and do not add a vowel.
Bring	Bringu	Do not drop tongue after making "g" sound.

Do Native English Speakers Cut the Endings of Some Words?

Yes, native speakers do change the endings of some words. As you learned in previous lessons, it is common for native speakers to blend sounds together. They sometimes blend the ending of a word with the beginning of another word. However, they are not deleting the sound. They are simply holding it and connecting it to the next word.

Are There Special Rules for Words Ending in "S" and "ED"?

Yes, there are three ways to pronounce words ending in "s" and three ways to pronounce words ending in "ed." Do you know the difference between the pronunciation of the following word endings?

"S" Endings	"ED" Endings
Types	Booked
Calls	Listened
Searches	Voted

Do not worry if you do not know the difference between these sounds. You will learn how to pronounce these words on pages 90 and 91.

> **REVIEW**
> Answer these questions without looking at the notes on the left.
>
> **Why are word endings important to hear?**
>
> **What kind of mistakes do nonnative speakers make with their word endings?**
>
> **Do native speakers ever cut off the endings of words?**
>
> **Are there special rules for words ending in "S" and "ED"?**

Goal for the Week: 3 Hrs

For audio, go to www.myovient.com and enter the audio code shown at the top of this page.

Word Endings (Holding Sounds) Audio #80590

Complete ☐

Practice holding onto the final consonant of these words for one second longer than you feel is natural. Read each word five times.

SOUNDS
CONNECTIONS
RHYTHM

NG ☐☐☐☐☐ giving ☐☐☐☐☐ wrong ☐☐☐☐☐ typing
☐☐☐☐☐ along ☐☐☐☐☐ calling ☐☐☐☐☐ preparing

S ☐☐☐☐☐ sounds ☐☐☐☐☐ pages ☐☐☐☐☐ changes
☐☐☐☐☐ phones ☐☐☐☐☐ glasses ☐☐☐☐☐ screens

SH ☐☐☐☐☐ establish ☐☐☐☐☐ slash ☐☐☐☐☐ clash
☐☐☐☐☐ distinguish ☐☐☐☐☐ brush ☐☐☐☐☐ wash

CH ☐☐☐☐☐ approach ☐☐☐☐☐ watch ☐☐☐☐☐ catch
☐☐☐☐☐ detach ☐☐☐☐☐ reach ☐☐☐☐☐ brunch

L ☐☐☐☐☐ tell ☐☐☐☐☐ sell ☐☐☐☐☐ annual
☐☐☐☐☐ hotel ☐☐☐☐☐ careful ☐☐☐☐☐ girl

R ☐☐☐☐☐ far ☐☐☐☐☐ never ☐☐☐☐☐ secure
☐☐☐☐☐ mirror ☐☐☐☐☐ our ☐☐☐☐☐ calendar

M ☐☐☐☐☐ team ☐☐☐☐☐ algorithm ☐☐☐☐☐ .com
☐☐☐☐☐ conform ☐☐☐☐☐ reform ☐☐☐☐☐ diagram

N ☐☐☐☐☐ can ☐☐☐☐☐ abandon ☐☐☐☐☐ down
☐☐☐☐☐ inspection ☐☐☐☐☐ fourteen ☐☐☐☐☐ men

V ☐☐☐☐☐ above ☐☐☐☐☐ evolve ☐☐☐☐☐ delve
☐☐☐☐☐ adaptive ☐☐☐☐☐ competitive ☐☐☐☐☐ executive

F ☐☐☐☐☐ stuff ☐☐☐☐☐ half ☐☐☐☐☐ spin-off
☐☐☐☐☐ bluff ☐☐☐☐☐ yourself ☐☐☐☐☐ cliff

TH ☐☐☐☐☐ tenth ☐☐☐☐☐ stealth ☐☐☐☐☐ wealth
☐☐☐☐☐ smooth ☐☐☐☐☐ loathe ☐☐☐☐☐ breathe

Practice Time Today:	Hrs	Min	**Practice Time this Week:**	Hrs	Min	**Goal for the Week: 3 Hrs**

For audio, go to www.myovient.com and enter the audio code shown at the top of this page.

Word Endings (Holding Sounds) Audio #80600

Complete

As you learned at the beginning of this book, it is important to stretch your word endings. This will help your English rhythm sound correct. In order to pronounce your word endings clearly, however, you also need to stretch the final consonant sounds.

☐ Read this paragraph and practice holding and stretching the final consonants that are underlined.

Opening up a large health club in Suntown was a risk for entrepreneur Trish Slaven. Although she had opened three other successful businesses, Ms. Slaven was unsure of the timing. The recession had hit the town hard, and many people were tightening their purse strings and didn't have extra money to spend. Her idea was met with skepticism by some business leaders, but she felt that a health club would be a great way for this community to improve their lives. She had three good reasons to open up a club. First, the only place to exercise was the rec center at the local college, and many people didn't feel comfortable working out with the students. Second, a recent influx of new residents had given the economy a boost. Third, the mayor was a former triathlete who supported her vision. Ms. Slaven opened the club and named it "Laps and Relax." It's been open six months. When asked about the club, Steph Brown, a member, raved, "It's a great place to work out. Sometimes I go there just to relax at the spa." It looks like Ms. Slaven made the right decision.

☐ ☐ **Read the paragraph two more times and record yourself. Listen to your recording and listen to your word endings. Can you hear the endings clearly?**

The best way to improve your pronunciation of word endings is to remind yourself to stretch the sounds at the ends of your words and to link your words together. Doing this will naturally improve your word-ending pronunciation.

☐ **Which word endings are difficult for you to hold? Write them down here and continue to practice.**

☐ **The next time you are speaking to a friend, tell her that you are working on improving your pronunciation of word endings. Ask her to let you know if you do not finish your words.**

| Practice Time Today: | Hrs | Min | **Practice Time this Week:** | Hrs | Min | **Goal for the Week: 3 Hrs** |

For audio, go to www.myovient.com and enter the audio code shown at the top of this page.

Word Endings (Consonant Clusters) Audio #80610 Complete ☐

☐ **Groups of consonant sounds are called consonant clusters. Read these clusters and practice clearly pronouncing all of the sounds in the clusters.**

SOUNDS
CONNECTIONS
RHYTHM

Ending in "p": -rp -sp -mp

Practice: ☐ warp ☐ sharp ☐ clasp ☐ wasp ☐ bump ☐ stump

Ending in "s": -ds -rs -ts -ps -rts -ves

Practice: ☐ attends ☐ adopters ☐ credits ☐ ships ☐ exports ☐ lives

Ending in "k" & "ks": -rk -nk -lk -sk -sks -ks

Practice: ☐ work ☐ think ☐ bulk ☐ ask ☐ asks ☐ attacks

Ending in "t": -rt -nt -ct -ft -pt -st

Practice: ☐ alert ☐ account ☐ affect ☐ draft ☐ accept ☐ receipt* ☐ first
(*The word receipt is irregular; the "p" is never pronounced.)

Ending in "th" & "ths": -nth -nths -fth -ths -thes

Practice: ☐ millionth ☐ months ☐ fifths ☐ youths ☐ bathes

Ending in "ch": -nch -rch -tch

Practice: ☐ launch ☐ search ☐ pitch ☐ crutch

Ending in "ing" & "ings": -ing -ings -inging

Practice: ☐ according ☐ buildings ☐ singing

Endings that blend with "r": -rf -rb -rn -rm -rd

Practice: ☐ turf ☐ blurb ☐ torn ☐ uniform ☐ word

☐ **Record yourself reading the paragraph from Lesson 6 Practice Day 5 (page 58). Focus on clearly pronouncing the word endings.**

Practice Time Today:	Hrs	Min	Practice Time this Week:	Hrs	Min	Goal for the Week: 3 Hrs

Word Endings (Single Consonants) Audio #80620   Complete ☐

Do not add an extra vowel to your consonant endings.

So far, you have practiced pronouncing ALL the sounds at the end of a word. It is important that you focus on this first because it is very easy for nonnative speakers to cut off the endings of words. However, you also need to be careful that you do not add an extra vowel sound to the ends of your words. Practice saying these words, but be careful not to include an extra vowel after the final consonant.

/iŋ/ not /iŋu/

☐ ☐ ☐ ☐ ☐ working   ☐ ☐ ☐ ☐ ☐ accounting   ☐ ☐ ☐ ☐ ☐ writing

☐ ☐ ☐ ☐ ☐ looking   ☐ ☐ ☐ ☐ ☐ analyzing   ☐ ☐ ☐ ☐ ☐ acting

/p/ not /pu/

☐ ☐ ☐ ☐ ☐ app   ☐ ☐ ☐ ☐ ☐ partnership   ☐ ☐ ☐ ☐ ☐ step

☐ ☐ ☐ ☐ ☐ rep   ☐ ☐ ☐ ☐ ☐ zip   ☐ ☐ ☐ ☐ ☐ wrap

/tʃ/ not /tʃi/

☐ ☐ ☐ ☐ ☐ March   ☐ ☐ ☐ ☐ ☐ switch   ☐ ☐ ☐ ☐ ☐ pitch

☐ ☐ ☐ ☐ ☐ church   ☐ ☐ ☐ ☐ ☐ itch   ☐ ☐ ☐ ☐ ☐ attach

/dʒ/ not /dʒi/

☐ ☐ ☐ ☐ ☐ judge   ☐ ☐ ☐ ☐ ☐ budge   ☐ ☐ ☐ ☐ ☐ garage

☐ ☐ ☐ ☐ ☐ converge   ☐ ☐ ☐ ☐ ☐ age   ☐ ☐ ☐ ☐ ☐ advantage

When words end in "e," the "e" is usually silent. These words end with a consonant sound.

☐ ☐ ☐ ☐ ☐ merge   ☐ ☐ ☐ ☐ ☐ life   ☐ ☐ ☐ ☐ ☐ ache

☐ ☐ ☐ ☐ ☐ strife   ☐ ☐ ☐ ☐ ☐ able   ☐ ☐ ☐ ☐ ☐ crave

However, sometimes the final "e" is pronounced.
1) When there is only one vowel: he, she, me
2) When the word ends in "ee": employee, trainee
3) When the "e" has an accent mark: café, résumé (The pronunciation is /eɪ/ not /i/.)

Pronunciation of Words Ending in "T"

Native English speakers often pronounce the letter "t" at the ends of words differently than the standard "t." A standard "t" is pronounced by holding your tongue against the top of your mouth, just behind your front teeth, and then dropping it quickly while blowing out a puff of air. Try it: *t, to*.

In word endings, however, that puff of air is often held and no sound is released. To practice this, finish the word with your tongue in the "t" position, but hold it there without dropping your tongue or releasing the puff of air. Try it: *at*.

☐ got   ☐ about   ☐ but   ☐ can't   ☐ client   ☐ front   ☐ start   ☐ market

---

Practice Time Today: ___ Hrs ___ Min   **Practice Time this Week:** ___ Hrs ___ Min   **Goal for the Week: 3 Hrs**

          For audio, go to www.myovient.com and enter the audio code shown at the top of this page.

Word Endings ("S" Endings) Audio #80630   Complete ☐

Do you pronounce the "s" endings in the following words differently: *Talks – Videos – Pages*? **You should. These sounds are different.**

There are three ways to pronounce the letter "s" at the ends of words:

```
SOUNDS
CONNECTIONS
RHYTHM
```

1. "S" is pronounced /s/ after unvoiced sounds.

looks   makes   talks   straps   apps   budgets   amounts

2. "S" is pronounced /z/ after voiced sounds.

films   pixels   tripods   cameras   files   frames   pictures

3. "S" is pronounced /ɪz/ after /s/, /z/, /ʃ/, /ʒ/, /tʃ/, /dʒ/ sounds. (This adds a syllable to the word.)

lenses   flashes   resizes   watches   poses   pages   advances

☐ **Look at this paragraph and underline or highlight all of the S endings you see. How is each "s" pronounced?**

When vacationers snap photos for their scrapbooks, they don't usually worry about lenses, flashes, or even the people's poses. They just "point and click." This style produces photos that are great for uploading to social networking sites, but without tripods, special lenses, and an eye for balance, these photos will definitely not become screen savers. Your family's poses in Times Square probably look just like your friends' photos. Professional photographers always look for scenes and poses that are unique. When professionals shoot a photo, they pay attention to the light, balance, and message that the image gives. With advances in cameras, everyday photographers can improve their images, but technology alone will not turn the hobbyists into professionals. To make that jump, amateurs need lessons, not better cameras.

☐ **Record yourself reading this paragraph. Can you clearly hear the letter "s" endings?**

Practice Time Today:		Hrs		Min	Practice Time this Week:		Hrs		Min	Goal for the Week: 3 Hrs

Word Endings ("ED" Endings) Audio #80640   Complete ☐

Do you pronounce the "ed" endings in the following words differently: *Watched – Showed – Added*? **You should. These sounds are different.**

There are three ways to pronounce the letters "ed" at the ends of words:

1. "Ed" is pronounced /t/ after unvoiced sounds.
searched   watched   passed   danced   washed   matched

2. "Ed" is pronounced /d/ after voiced sounds.
grabbed   arrived   breathed   bored   ruined   showed

3. "Ed" is pronounced as /ɪd/ after /t/ or /d/. (This adds a syllable to the word.)
needed   wanted   suggested   added   depended   visited

☐ **Look at this paragraph and underline or highlight all of the "ed" endings you see. How is each "ed" pronounced?**

Enid was an engineer noted for her research in computer network security systems. Although she often analyzed complicated attacks on computers, the security system for her house baffled her. When she first installed her own alarm system, she avoided turning it on because it beeped at regular intervals and bothered her. She believed that a system wasn't needed for her house. She felt her neighborhood was safe. But after hearing that a thief had climbed through a neighbor's back window and robbed him of $500, she finally asked a technician for help. An alarm system rep visited her house and realized that Enid had bought such a complicated system that it was nearly impossible to use every day. He changed some settings and customized her system so that it could be controlled from her computer. She cheered at that news because she felt more comfortable using her computer than the control box that had been installed in her home. After the tech fixed it, she thanked him and offered to give him a free security upgrade for his computer. He declined because he claimed he didn't need computer security. She was astonished, but understood…she used to think the same thing about her home security!

☐ **Record yourself reading this paragraph. Can you clearly hear the ED endings?**

Linking and Word Endings Review

Complete ☐

☐ **Find a book, magazine or article on the Internet and read a paragraph aloud. Make sure it is something that you have never read before. Pay attention to your word endings. Record yourself. Are all of your word endings clear?**

☐ **Listen to your recording while reading along with the paragraph. Circle any word endings on the page that you feel you did not pronounce clearly. Read it again and record it. Listen and check your pronunciation again.**

☐ **Read the paragraph from the previous exercise one more time. This time pay close attention to your pausing. Make sure you are adding pauses between the phrases. Remember to add rhythm to your speech even when you are practicing your sounds!**

SOUNDS
CONNECTIONS
RHYTHM

Self-Reflection:

Write your feelings about your pronunciation improvement so far. Have you received any feedback about your pronunciation from friends or coworkers since you started this program?

_____

_____

_____

_____

_____

_____

_____

_____

| **Practice Time Today:** | Hrs | Min | **Practice Time this Week:** | Hrs | Min | **Goal for the Week: 3 Hrs** |

Noise and Review

SOUNDS
CONNECTIONS
RHYTHM

What Is Noise?

Have you ever tried to talk on the phone with someone in a noisy room? Or, have you ever tried to have a quiet conversation with someone in a loud restaurant? It is difficult to focus on someone's speech when there is a lot of noise around you. The same thing happens when you add extra or unnecessary words or sounds to your language. It creates noise. Look at this speech:

A. Uh, Good afternoon. Um, thanks for coming to this uh meeting. Um, I'd like to uh begin by uh letting you know that um it's uh very important that uh we get this um project finished uh by the uh end of the quarter.

Compare it with this speech:

B. Good afternoon. Thanks for coming to this meeting. I'd like to begin by letting you know that it's very important that we get this project finished by the end of the quarter.

Speech "B" is much clearer, and the speaker sounds more confident and trustworthy.

Why Is Noise Bad for Clear Speech?

Noise makes it difficult for people to hear your important words. People might focus more on your noise than on your key words. These extra sounds also make you appear nervous or unsure of your topic.

How Do I Know If I Have 'Noise' in My Speech?

First, ask your friends or coworkers if there are expressions, words, or sounds that you overuse while speaking. Tell them to be totally honest with you!

Second, record yourself speaking in different situations. Listen to the recording. Make a list of non-essential sounds, words, and phrases that you frequently use. These might include phrases such as "let's see" or "you know."

How Can I Eliminate Noise?

First, you need to understand how much noise you have in your speech. Have someone count how many times you use a particular word or phrase in a given time period. For example, ask a coworker to count how many "you knows" or "uhs" you say in a presentation.

Second, write the word you want to avoid on a note card and place it somewhere you will see it often. Set up phone or calendar reminders to pop up and remind you to avoid this word. When you notice yourself saying this word or phrase often, allow yourself to pause and be quiet instead of saying the word. Over time, you will train yourself to use a silent pause instead of the word.

Native Speakers Have 'Noise' in Their Speech, Why Can't I?

Yes, it is true. Even native speakers have noise in their speech. However, a good speaker avoids excess noise in their speech, regardless of their first language. Native speakers need speech training too!

Lesson 11 / Practice Day 1

Noise and Review Audio #80650　　　　　　　　　　　　　Complete ☐

☐ **Read the following speech exactly as it is written. Record yourself and listen to your recording. Did you notice how the noise makes the meaning unclear? This is not the way you should speak!**

SOUNDS
CONNECTIONS
RHYTHM

Umm, "Innovation" is uh, a popular buzzword today. You know, companies claim that their products are, umm, innovative, uh, business leaders say that, you know, the key to success is, uh, innovation, and everyday workers know that innovation could, uh, help them get a promotion. I mean, if innovation is the key, is the key to our, um, success, then we should be, we should be focusing all of our attention on it, right? However, you know, if we're honest with ourselves, we're not, umm, spending much time on our own innovation, are we? Being innovative, um, doesn't necessarily take a lot of, umm, money. Instead, it takes a, uh, uh, a paradigm shift. In order to, umm, innovate, we need to look at our, umm, life and, umm, daily work tasks and say, this isn't, uh, working well.

☐ **Read the paragraph and pause when you see brackets [ ]. This indicates where the noise was in the previous reading. A short pause is better than adding noise!**

[　] "Innovation" is [　] a popular buzzword today. [　] companies claim that their products are [　] innovative, [　] business leaders say that [　] the key to success is [　] innovation, and everyday workers know that innovation could [　] help them get a promotion. [　] If innovation is the key [　] to our [　] success, then we should be [　] focusing all of our attention on it, right? However, [　] if we're honest with ourselves, we're not [　] spending much time on our own innovation, are we? Being innovative [　] doesn't necessarily take a lot of [　] money. Instead, it takes [　] a paradigm shift. In order to [　] innovate, we need to look at our [　] life and [　] daily work tasks and say, this isn't [　] working well. What can I do to [　] improve it?

Review:
Read the paragraph again without pausing at the brackets, and focus on ONE skill from this book. What skill will you review? _____

Practice Time Today:	Hrs	Min	**Practice Time this Week:**	Hrs	Min	**Goal for the Week: 3 Hrs**

Noise and Review

What is your most common 'noise'? This activity will help you find out.

1. Speak for one minute about the topics listed in the table below. Record yourself, listen to it, and count how many times you repeat a specific sound or word. Write the information in the table below.

2. Speak again for one minute about the same topic and try to avoid saying the word that you wrote down in the 'noise' column. Record it, play it back, and fill in the table with the number of times you said the word you were trying to avoid.

3. Finally, speak again for one minute on the same topic and try to eliminate your "noise" again. In addition, focus on reviewing a pronunciation principle from this book. Write down the principle in the column on the right. Record it and listen to yourself. Did you avoid adding noise? Did you correctly use the pronunciation principle you chose?

Follow the examples in this table:

Topic	Noise (you know, uh, umm, see, eh, like)	Frequency (# of times)	Pronunciation Review
Ex 1. Innovation	umm	7	
Ex 2. Innovation	umm	3	
Ex 3. Innovation	umm	1	Word Endings
1. Travel			
2. Travel			
3. Travel			
1. Meetings			
2. Meetings			
3. Meetings			
1. Public Speaking			
2. Public Speaking			
3. Public Speaking			

Practice Time Today: Hrs Min **Practice Time this Week:** Hrs Min **Goal for the Week: 3 Hrs**

  For audio, go to www.myovient.com and enter the audio code shown at the top of this page.

Lesson 11 / Practice Day 3

Noise and Review

Complete ☐

Personal Speech

☐ **Use the outline below to prepare a quick speech. Record yourself giving the speech. Look at yourself in the mirror while giving it. You may look at your notes occasionally, but do not read directly from your notes while giving the speech.**

SOUNDS
CONNECTIONS
RHYTHM

Title: <u>One Memorable Day In My Life</u>

Introduction:

What happened on that day?

Conclusion:

☐ **Listen to your recording. Ask a friend or teacher to listen and give you feedback.**

Did you add any extra noise? What kind? _____

What areas of pronunciation do you think you need to continue to practice? _____

☐ **Give the speech again and focus on incorporating 'pauses' between your thought groups.**

Did you add any extra noise? What kind? _____

Did you use "pausing" in your speech? _____

Practice Time Today:	Hrs	Min	Practice Time this Week:	Hrs	Min	Goal for the Week: 3 Hrs

Noise and Review

Complete ☐

How-To Speech

☐ **Use the outline below to prepare a quick speech. Record yourself giving the speech. Look at yourself in the mirror while giving it. You may look at your notes occasionally, but do not read directly from your notes while giving the speech.**

SOUNDS
CONNECTIONS
RHYTHM

Title: How to _____(Write the name of a task, like "make coffee.")

Introduction:

What are the steps?

Conclusion:

☐ **Listen to your recording. Ask a friend or teacher to listen and give you feedback.**

Did you add any extra noise? What kind? _____

What areas of pronunciation do you think you need to continue to practice? _____

☐ **Give the speech again and focus on adding 'connections' between your words.**

Did you add any extra noise? What kind? _____

Did you use "connections" in your speech? _____

| **Practice Time Today:** | Hrs | Min | **Practice Time this Week:** | Hrs | Min | **Goal for the Week: 3 Hrs** |

For audio, go to www.myovient.com and enter the audio code shown at the top of this page.

Noise and Review

Complete ▢

Job Interview Questions

SOUNDS
CONNECTIONS
RHYTHM

▢ **Imagine you are in a job interview. Answer these questions and focus on avoiding all noise. When you answer questions in an interview, you need to look CONFIDENT and RELAXED. If you have noise in your speech, you will look neither confident nor relaxed. Record your answers.**

Tips

If you do not know how to answer a question, you can give yourself extra time by:

- restating the question
- asking for clarification
- telling a story that explains your experience with the topic
- using phrases like "Let me see" or "That's a good question"
- speaking slowly and carefully (Speaking too quickly will force you to say more.)

Questions (Be sure to record your answers.)

1) Describe your current job.

2) What kind of job position are you looking for?

3) Are you a team player?

4) Why do you think you are the best candidate for this job?

5) What are your long-term goals?

6) What is one thing that you want us to know about you that's not on your resume?

▢ **Listen to your recording. Also, ask a friend or teacher to listen and give you feedback.**

What did you notice about your pronunciation?

Did you speak carefully without noise?

Did you pause between thought groups?

Where there any sounds that were difficult to understand?

Practice Time Today:	Hrs	Min	**Practice Time this Week:**	Hrs	Min	**Goal for the Week: 3 Hrs**

Noise and Review

Complete ☐

Business Communication Situations

☐ **Record yourself completing the tasks below. Focus on speaking clearly with no noise. Also, try to pronounce individual sounds correctly. Pay careful attention to sounds that are difficult for you.**

Task 1: Jane is a new employee at your company. You are showing her where the kitchen is and you run into another employee, Todd. Introduce Jane to Todd.

Task 2: You are the facilitator at a meeting at your company. Everyone has arrived and is participating in some pre-meeting small talk. Get everyone's attention and start the meeting.

Task 3: You are at your company's annual picnic. The president of the company had to take an urgent phone call and cannot give the welcome speech. Give a short welcome speech to everyone there.

Task 4: People are complaining about the automated voicemail message on your telephone because it is not your voice. Record a new outgoing message.

☐ **Listen to your recordings and practice again if you feel that you need to improve. Ask a friend or teacher to listen and give you feedback.**

What sounds do you still need to improve?

What words did you have trouble pronouncing?

Did you avoid extra noise?

Did you remember to add intonation to your voice?

Did you remember to stress your key words?

Practice Time Today: ___ Hrs ___ Min   **Practice Time this Week:** ___ Hrs ___ Min   **Goal for the Week: 3 Hrs**

For audio, go to www.myovient.com and enter the audio code shown at the top of this page.

Lesson 11 / Practice Day 7

Review

Complete

Answer these questions without looking at your notes. You can check your answers by reviewing the lesson that is written in parentheses after each question.

SOUNDS
CONNECTIONS
RHYTHM

☐ What are thought groups, and why are they important? (LESSON 1)

☐ Where should you stretch your words? (LESSON 2)

☐ Which individual words in a sentence should be stressed? (LESSON 4)

☐ What words have a rising intonation when you are asking an informational question? (LESSON 5)

☐ What happens to the pronunciation of unstressed syllables in words? (LESSON 6)

☐ How do words link together? (LESSONS 3 and 7)

☐ Why are native English speakers difficult to understand when they speak casually? (LESSON 8)

☐ What individual sounds are difficult for you? (LESSON 9)

☐ What are the pronunciation rules for words ending in "s"? (LESSON 10)

Record yourself reading the paragraph below, and compare it to your recording from the beginning of this program (page 5). Play your two recordings to a friend or teacher and ask if he or she can hear a difference.

Do you ever look around you and wonder whether you are dressed appropriately for your job? Do you notice men coming to work without a tie and think they're underdressed? Dress codes in many companies today are relaxed, and in many cases "business-casual" clothing is normal. Khaki pants and shirts without ties are common and acceptable. This is especially true in professions where employees are not in face-to-face contact with customers. Some employees in more relaxed areas of business can even go to work in jeans and t-shirts. Even if their workplace requires more formal clothing, like suits and ties, they might have one day a week when employees can relax and dress down, usually called "casual Friday." The best way to understand how to dress for your workplace is to analyze what your coworkers are wearing. Whatever your company requires, be sure to wear clothing that feels good. That way, even if you don't like the dress code, at least you'll be comfortable!

| Practice Time Today: | Hrs | Min | Practice Time this Week: | Hrs | Min | Goal for the Week: 3 Hrs |

©2013 Ovient, Inc. All rights reserved.

Questions People Ask about Pronunciation

Should my mouth change shape when I speak English?

Yes. As you speak English, the shape of your mouth should be different than when you speak your native language. Speaking English will actually FEEL different! You may want to look in a mirror when you are practicing your English pronunciation so you can see the difference.

Open your mouth! English has many different sounds that require you to open your mouth wide. Opening your mouth wide when you speak will help you pronounce difficult sounds and pronounce them clearly. Do you open your mouth wide enough? Your teeth should show when you are speaking!

Not even close!   Better, but still too narrow.   Much better!

Is there anything I can do to master a difficult sound?

You may find that it helps to move your head, hands, or even your whole body when you are practicing pronunciation. You can move up on your toes to help you raise your pitch or use your hand to copy the movement of your tongue when pronouncing an "r" or "th." You can use body movements when you practice and even when you are speaking to other people. The movements may seem big to you, but other people will probably not notice them. Do not worry. You will not have to continue to do this forever—just until you have mastered the sound.

If you are having trouble pronouncing a sound, pay attention to where your tongue is in your mouth, what shape your lips are making, and whether or not you are using your vocal cords. Ask a native speaker to make the sound and describe what is happening inside his or her mouth. Ask him or her to help you understand what you are doing wrong.

You need to practice a sound hundreds of times in order to master it. You should practice the sound at least a few times every day until you feel totally comfortable using it.

When will I see results?

Changing habits that you have had for many years takes time and patience. However, once you understand your most important pronunciation problems and take steps to change, you can see results immediately. Typically, changing your pronunciation takes three steps: **awareness**, **practice** and **use**. First, you must become **aware** of your mistakes and learn to correct them. Then, you must **practice** with drills and exercises to re-train your muscles and form new habits. Finally, you must **use** these principles in your everyday speech. While most people do not see change overnight, if you do all of the assignments and make a strong effort to use these principles in daily conversation, you will improve.

Most people notice that their pronunciation has improved when other people start to interact with them differently. When you notice that your coworkers talk with you more often and ask you to repeat yourself less frequently, and you have an easier time talking with people over the phone, you will know you have improved.

American English IPA (International Phonetic Alphabet) Audio #80660

The phonetic alphabet is a useful tool when you are studying pronunciation. Each of the symbols in the IPA represent a unique sound in the English language. The symbols below represent the sounds you need to know in order to speak American English.

You do not need to worry about memorizing the pronunciation symbols immediately, but eventually you will find that understanding the IPA and the pronunciation symbols used by your dictionary will help you quickly understand how to pronounce new words correctly.

Consonants	
Symbol	Sound it Represents
s	security
z	zoom
ʃ	flash
ʒ	measure
t	turn
ʔ	button
d	modern
tʃ	chip
dʒ	just
p	profit
b	benefit
f	format
v	virtual
θ	think
ð	this
k	cable
g	grant
m	motor
n	new
ŋ	ring
l	light
r	right
w	would
j	yell
h	how

Vowels	
Symbol	Sound it Represents
i	meeting
ɪ	Internet
ɛ	edge
æ	app
ɑ	processor
ɔ	caught
u	virtual
ʊ	would
ə	account
ʌ	cut
eɪ	make
aɪ	client
aʊ	however
ɔɪ	noise
oʊ	know

Lungs, Vocal Cords, Tongue, Teeth, Lips, and Nose

As you speak, air passes from your lungs through your vocal cords, past your tongue and teeth, and out your mouth. The shape of your mouth, the position of your tongue, the position of your teeth and lips, and whether you vibrate your vocal cords all work together to create a unique sound.

Phonetic Alphabet Study Chart with Reference Words

Write down a reference word that will help you remember each sound in the English language. Your reference word should be a word that contains the sound and is easy for you to pronounce. In the future, if you forget how to pronounce a sound, you can use your reference word to help you remember.

Consonants		
Symbol	Sample Word	Your Reference Word
s	security	
z	zoom	
ʃ	flash	
ʒ	measure	
t	turn	
ʔ	button	
d	modern	
tʃ	chip	
dʒ	just	
p	profit	
b	benefit	
f	format	
v	virtual	
θ	think	
ð	this	
k	cable	
g	grant	
m	motor	
n	new	
ŋ	ring	
l	light	
r	right	
w	would	
j	yell	
h	how	

Vowels		
Symbol	Sample Word	Your Reference Word
i	meeting	
ɪ	Internet	
ɛ	edge	
æ	app	
ɑ	processor	
ɔ	caught	
u	virtual	
ʊ	would	
ə	account	
ʌ	cut	
eɪ	make	
aɪ	client	
aʊ	however	
ɔɪ	noise	
oʊ	know	

Word List Study Sheet

Write down words that you need to practice pronouncing. Cross off the word when you can consistently pronounce it correctly in your daily speech. (Ask a teacher or friend to guide you.)

Word	Phonetic Spelling	Tips for Pronouncing

Word List Study Sheet

Write down words that you need to practice pronouncing. Cross off the word when you can consistently pronounce it correctly in your daily speech. (Ask a teacher or friend to guide you.)

Word	Phonetic Spelling	Tips for Pronouncing

For audio, go to www.myovient.com and enter the audio code shown at the top of this page.

Speaker Role Models

Think of two people who have a way of speaking that you like. Try to think of two people who speak clearly and confidently. One should be someone you know personally, such as a coworker, manager, or friend. The other could be a politician, religious figure, celebrity, or world leader. Paste a photo of each person below. What do you like about the speech style of these two people? Use the categories below to help you analyze their speech.

Person 1:

Person 2:

Speed of Speech
Does this person speak slowly or quickly?

Person 1:

Person 2:

Voice Pitch
Does this person have a low voice or a high voice? Does this person change his/her voice pitch when speaking?

Person 1:

Person 2:

Voice Tone
Does this person have a strong or soft voice? When this person is speaking, can you hear him/her clearly?

Person 1:

Person 2:

Body Language
What body language and gestures does this person use when speaking? Does this person make eye contact with his/her audience?

Person 1:

Person 2

Use of Silence/Pausing
How does this person use silence when he/she speaks? Does this person pause frequently when speaking?

Person 1:

Person 2:

Clear Speech
Is this person easy to understand? Why or why not?

Person 1:

Person 2:

The Perfect You!

Now, imagine that you have acquired the best skills of both of your role models. Paste a photo of *yourself* below. Write your favorite skills from each of your role models in the sections next to your photo. Imagine that you are this amazing speaker and that you have all of these skills. Act like this person. Become this person. This is you!

You!

Body Language (gestures, facial expressions, eye contact)

Use of Silence/Pausing

Speed of Speech (fast, slow, or varied)

Clear Speech

Voice Pitch (high, low, or varied)

Voice Tone (soft or harsh)

Other thoughts:

Pronunciation Warm-Ups Audio #80670

Do these exercises any time you need to warm up your mouth or voice.
Memorize the words and sounds so that you can practice them anywhere.

Breathing & Stretching Exercises

- Sit up straight with both feet flat on the floor. Place your hands on your lap.
- Take a deep breath through your nose. Hold it for 3 seconds.
- Release the air forcefully through your mouth, dropping your shoulders.
- Open your mouth wide as if you are going to yawn.
- Hold your mouth open for 3 seconds and close it.
- Massage the corners of your jaw with your hands and allow the jaw to relax and open.

Sound Exercises

Repeat these sounds as quickly as you can. Stress the bolded sounds.

ba-da-ga-da – **ba**-da-ga-da – **ba**-da-ga-da – **ba**-da-ga-da – **ba**-da-ga-da – **ba**-da-ga-da – **ba**

ga-da-ba-da – **ga**-da-ba-da – **ga**-da-ba-da – **ga**-da-ba-da – **ga**-da-ba-da – **ga**-da-ba-da – **ga**

pa-ta-ka-ta – **pa**-ta-ka-ta – **pa**-ta-ka-ta – **pa**-ta-ka-ta – **pa**-ta-ka-ta – **pa**-ta-ka-ta – **pa**-ta-ka-ta – **pa**

ka-ta-pa-ta – **ka**-ta-pa-ta – **ka**-ta-pa-ta – **ka**-ta-pa-ta – **ka**-ta-pa-ta – **ka**-ta-pa-ta – **ka**-ta-pa-ta – **ka**

va-la-wa-la – **va**-la-wa-la – **va**-la-wa-la – **va**-la-wa-la – **va**-la-wa-la – **va**-la-wa-la – **va**-la-wa-la – **va**

wa-la-va-la – **wa**-la-va-la – **wa**-la-va-la – **wa**-la-va-la – **wa**-la-va-la – **wa**-la-va-la – **wa**-la-va-la – **wa**

Tongue Twisters

Repeat each sentence three times as fast as you can.

☐ ☐ ☐ Walt wondered if Vern valued the wonderful violets in the window.

☐ ☐ ☐ The leisure ledger was a pleasure to measure.

☐ ☐ ☐ Lee never laughed a lot like Lou's nephew.

☐ ☐ ☐ Shelby the Schnauzer was chastised for chewing the shoe.

☐ ☐ ☐ ROFL means 'rolling on the floor laughing.'

Rhythm Exercises

Read the poem. Stress the bold words and pause at the slashes.

There **once** was a de**vel**oper named **Bob**, / who **could**n't find **joy** in his **job**. / He **want**ed to **quit** / but he **could**n't ad**mit** / that he **did** / love to **hear** / himself **sob**.

Intonation Exercises

Raise the pitch of your voice on each word that is underlined.

I <u>will</u> make <u>my</u> voice <u>change</u> at <u>this</u> time.

<u>I</u> will <u>make</u> my <u>voice</u> change <u>at</u> this <u>time</u>.

I will <u>make</u> my <u>voice</u> change at <u>this</u> time.

Continued on next page

Pronunciation Warm-Ups Continued Audio #80670

Stress Exercises to Change Your Focus
Stress each word that is in bold.

What have you been doing?
What **have** you been doing?
What have **you** been doing?
What have you **been** doing?
What have you been **doing**?

Pausing Exercises
Pause at each slash.

Changing directions / at this point / would just set us back / six months.

Stretching Exercises
Stretch the word endings at the end of each phrase.

I would have call--------ed, but I wasn't su------re if it was a good idea----------.

Connecting Exercises
Connect the words together.

It'snotagoodidea / tospendthatmuchmoney / onanadvertisement.

Further Study

Congratulations on finishing the Ovient Accent Diet™!

Now that you have learned and practiced the principles of American English pronunciation, you need to keep practicing. Just like with a food diet, the Accent Diet™ requires you to keep using the skills you have learned so that they become part of your daily life. Your old habits will return if you do not make a conscious effort to maintain your new habits.

Improving your pronunciation takes more than brain power. You need practice—lots of it!

First, remind yourself of the areas of pronunciation that you need to work on:

- Are you pausing between your thought groups? Do you talk too quickly or too slowly?

- Are you stretching the endings of your thought groups? Are you stressing the correct syllables in your words and the correct key words in your sentences?

- Are you pronouncing the endings of your words clearly?

- What individual sounds do you need to continue to practice?

Second, practice:

- Write a reminder on a sticky note and put it where you will see it every day (on your computer, refrigerator, car dashboard, etc.).

- Set a reminder on your phone or calendar to remind yourself to practice a particular sound or skill at different times of the day or week.

- Use a daily task to remind yourself to work on a skill. For example, every time you wash your hands, practice a sound.

- Talk to yourself! Speak as much as possible, even when you are alone.

Next, check yourself:

- Once a month, record yourself talking and listen to it to see if your pronunciation is clear.

- Ask a trustworthy friend to give you honest feedback on your pronunciation.

Finally, be proud and show off your skills:

- Volunteer to give presentations at work and show others how well you speak.

- Join networking and other social groups and interact with other English speakers.

- Teach other nonnative English speakers how to improve their pronunciation!

Further Study: Retaining Your New Pronunciation Skills

In the topic column in the table below, write the areas of pronunciation that you want to keep practicing. Write the date in the "week" boxes when you complete a review activity.

For the first month after you complete this program, spend a little time once a week reviewing.

Topic	Week 1	Week 2	Week 3	Week 4
ex) Stretching: read a word list & practiced stretching	Feb. 2	Feb. 9	Feb. 16	Feb. 23

In the second month, spend a little time once every two weeks reviewing.

Topic	Week 6	Week 8	Week 10	Week 12

In the next four months, you should review once a month. Keep reviewing as long as necessary.

Topic	Week 16	Week 20	Week 24	Week 28

Notes

Notes

For audio, go to www.myovient.com and enter the audio code shown at the top of this page.

Made in the USA
San Bernardino, CA
10 February 2018